TEQUILA

Edible

Series Editor: Andrew F. Smith

EDIBLE is a revolutionary series of books dedicated to food and drink that explores the rich history of cuisine. Each book reveals the global history and culture of one type of food or beverage.

Already published

Apple Erika Janik, *Avocado* Jeff Miller, *Banana* Lorna Piatti-Farnell, *Barbecue* Jonathan Deutsch and Megan J. Elias, *Beans* Nathalie Rachel Morris, *Beef* Lorna Piatti-Farnell, *Beer* Gavin D. Smith, *Berries* Heather Arndt Anderson, *Biscuits and Cookies* Anastasia Edwards, *Brandy* Becky Sue Epstein, *Bread* William Rubel, *Cabbage* Meg Muckenhoupt, *Cake* Nicola Humble, *Caviar* Nichola Fletcher, *Champagne* Becky Sue Epstein, *Cheese* Andrew Dalby, *Chillies* Heather Arndt Anderson, *Chocolate* Sarah Moss and Alexander Badenoch, *Cocktails* Joseph M. Carlin, *Coffee* Jonathan Morris, *Corn* Michael Owen Jones, *Curry* Colleen Taylor Sen, *Dates* Nawal Nasrallah, *Doughnut* Heather Delancey Hunwick, *Dumplings* Barbara Gallani, *Edible Flowers* Constance L. Kirker and Mary Newman, *Edible Insects* Gina Louise Hunter, *Eggs* Diane Toops, *Fats* Michelle Phillipov, *Figs* David C. Sutton, *Foie Gras* Norman Kolpas, *Game* Paula Young Lee, *Gin* Lesley Jacobs Solmonson, *Hamburger* Andrew F. Smith, *Herbs* Gary Allen, *Herring* Kathy Hunt, *Honey* Lucy M. Long, *Hot Dog* Bruce Kraig, *Hummus* Harriet Nussbaum, *Ice Cream* Laura B. Weiss, *Jam, Jelly and Marmalade* Sarah B. Hood, *Lamb* Brian Yarvin, *Lemon* Toby Sonneman, *Lobster* Elisabeth Townsend, *Melon* Sylvia Lovegren, *Milk* Hannah Velten, *Moonshine* Kevin R. Kosar, *Mushroom* Cynthia D. Bertelsen, *Mustard* Demet Güzey, *Nuts* Ken Albala, *Offal* Nina Edwards, *Olive* Fabrizia Lanza, *Onions and Garlic* Martha Jay, *Oranges* Clarissa Hyman, *Oyster* Carolyn Tillie, *Pancake* Ken Albala, *Pasta and Noodles* Kantha Shelke, *Pickles* Jan Davison, *Pie* Janet Clarkson, *Pineapple* Kaori O'Connor, *Pizza* Carol Helstosky, *Pomegranate* Damien Stone, *Pork* Katharine M. Rogers, *Potato* Andrew F. Smith, *Pudding* Jeri Quinzio, *Rice* Renee Marton, *Rum* Richard Foss, *Saffron* Ramin Ganeshram, *Salad* Judith Weinraub, *Salmon* Nicolaas Mink, *Sandwich* Bee Wilson, *Sauces* Maryann Tebben, *Sausage* Gary Allen, *Seaweed* Kaori O'Connor, *Shrimp* Yvette Florio Lane, *Soda and Fizzy Drinks* Judith Levin, *Soup* Janet Clarkson, *Spices* Fred Czarra, *Sugar* Andrew F. Smith, *Sweets and Candy* Laura Mason, *Tea* Helen Saberi, *Tequila* Ian Williams, *Tomato* Clarissa Hyman, *Truffle* Zachary Nowak, *Vanilla* Rosa Abreu-Runkel, *Vodka* Patricia Herlihy, *Water* Ian Miller, *Whiskey* Kevin R. Kosar, *Wine* Marc Millon, *Yoghurt* June Hersh

Tequila

A Global History

Ian Williams

REAKTION BOOKS

To Dori Bryant, Juan Bernardo Torres Mora, Doug French,
Martin Grassl and all the others who helped me imbibe
so much material for my research

Published by Reaktion Books Ltd
Unit 32, Waterside
44–48 Wharf Road
London N1 7UX, UK
www.reaktionbooks.co.uk

First published 2015, reprinted 2021

Printed and bound in India by Replika Press Pvt. Ltd

A catalogue record for this book is available
from the British Library

ISBN 978 1 78023 435 9

Contents

Foreword

Drinking spirits is an acquired habit. Although distilled alcohol is an admirably effective and speedy way to convey a buzz to the blood and brain, it often hits the palate with an initial harshness that is not immediately conducive to refined sensory gratification. That is why, over the centuries, drinkers invented cocktails, punches, liqueurs and myriad other ways to smooth the path of strong liquor down delicate throats. There is also an alternative method: quickly gulping down shots to expedite the passage of the stuff past the senses of smell and taste.

One big advantage of distilled spirits is their portability. Spirits not only need less storage space, but will not go sour as beers or wines sometimes do. They were historically usually drunk diluted anyway, in punches and similar cocktails, so concentrating them is done as much for reasons of commercial convenience as for taste. It is much easier to ship a barrel of spirits than to tote the ten or so casks that would be needed to transport the equivalent amount of alcohol within fermented drinks, which in turn is easier than moving the tons of barley, grapes, corn or agave used to begin the process.

For centuries, small quantities were distilled in monasteries and apothecaries and used as *aqua vitae* – the water of life, treasured for its revivifying effect on the sick. Even though many surviving patients would have drunk to its therapeutic effect, our palate usually needs training to take spirits neat or to tolerate and relish the oaky flavours that the ageing process gives to most brown spirits, the smoky aroma of single malts or the peppery tingle from the agave that tequila and mescal communicate to the sides of the tongue, along with the hints of smoke from the roasting of the pods.

It symbolizes the triumph of the human spirit that we overcome our initial adverse reactions and persevere to savour the complexities and subtleties of the distiller's art, and indeed come to cherish them so fondly. Perhaps more well than wisely, I have appreciated Chinese *maotai*, Balkan slivovitz and raki, Indian 'country liquor' and Haitian *clairin*, 'white lightning' moonshine from the Appalachians and even Irish poteen, which had intriguing rubbery notes since it had been smuggled through the Liverpool docks in the inner tubes of spare wheels on trucks coming off the Irish Sea ferries.

Like most casual tequila drinkers, my first acquaintances with Mexico's gift to a grateful world came buffered with other ingredients in large frozen margaritas. My friend Winston Cole was the bar manager at Zarela's restaurant in midtown Manhattan, which combined exquisite Oaxacan cuisine with a rapidly flowing glacier of frozen margaritas. In the late 1990s he served huge, heaped glasses of them to seething masses of bent brokers celebrating their ill-gotten gains from hawking dubious shares to gullible investors. Winston usually imposed a limit of three frozen margaritas per customer, and his policy was more than vindicated one night when we noticed a couple making love while standing up in the middle of the seething crowd. It was powerful stuff.

With emblazoned numbers that were more suggestive than significant, the tequila labels on Winston's bar shelves implied

Frozen margarita – most people's gateway drink to tequila.

years of ageing to the same levels as cognac and single-malt whisky. I checked and had to disillusion him: 'When it says twenty-one on the bottle, it might be the age of the distiller's daughter when she was married – but that's at least nineteen years older than the contents.'

However, while remaining popular, the idea of tequila as the drink of college binges, as epitomized in the old quip, 'Tequila! Have you hugged your toilet yet?', was being superseded as both product and palates became more refined. Aficionados were drinking it neat, not only as machismo-manifesting shots, but as a fine liquor. Bars saw less of the salt and lime ritual that hid the shock of bad tequila.

First the tequila-makers or *tequileros*, and then later the *mezcaleros*, saw which way the liquor was flowing. Bulk sales of knock'em back tequilas were indeed *good* business, but the prices commanded by single malts, fine bourbons and cognacs sug-gested that fine, premium tequilas would be *superb* business. Ironically it was foreigners who pioneered the drive up the value chain, with Patrón and Porfidio in particular breaking into new niche markets. As we will see later, the Austrian entrepreneur behind Porfidio paid a heavy price for upsetting the pride of Mexican *tequileros*, even if they later followed the trail he had pioneered.

Much of the early campaign to raise the social standing of tequila concentrated on distinguishing it from mescal. Even now articles about tequila often feel the need to 'disambiguate' by stressing that tequila *never* has a 'worm' in it. But the new premium tequilas of the 1990s went further. They were not to be disguised with salt and citrus or ready-made Margarita mixes, let alone squishy talking points like pickled caterpillars. Nor were they to be thrown down quickly like medicine.

Now distillers are offering seven-year-old tequilas and mescals, the product of careful research on how to marry the smoothness that ageing brings to a spirit with the surprisingly delicate flavour of the agave. Discerning drinkers nose and relish them like the other premium spirits, letting the vapours waft around the palate, and savouring the multiple different components of the taste rolling around the tongue.

Years behind, but catching up, mescal has been following in tequila's wobbly footsteps to premium status. While some mescals still have a worm – not to mention other creeping crawling things – in the bottle, they too are moving upmarket. Makers sometimes need to stress that there is no connection whatsoever between mescal and the hallucinogenic mescal, or *peyotl*, fungus. Even now, some drinkers believe the myth that mescal produces hallucinations. While that might have some appeal to a certain kind of customer, *mezcaleros* hope that the distinctive qualities of premium mescals will attract a more discriminating, higher-paying type of drinker.

Well-attended festivals such as Dori Bryant's 'Spirits of Mexico' taught me and many others what was now available, but it was in the distilleries of Jalisco and Oaxaca that I really came to appreciate the subtle miracles that can result from fermenting and distilling the pods of the agave plant. With expert tuition and coaching from stillmasters, I picked up the complex nuances that could otherwise easily be overlooked, not least when approached with acquired prejudices.

I also began to appreciate the dedication of *tequileros* and *mezcaleros*. For them, the result of their work was much more than a mere drink. It was the distilled essence of Mexican tradition – a patriotic and indeed spiritual experience. In the corners of distilleries workers always placed small shrines with icons of the local saints, who, in the nature of Mexican religiosity, often seemed to be pagan gods dressed in a veneer of Christian finery and continued an ancient tradition of linking the agave, or *maguey*, and its products with the divine.

Whether they used stainless-steel autoclaves or open fire pits, mechanical mills or troughs with mallets, the distillers I met were totally committed to their products. They had widely different views on everything from the different ways of trimming the agave pods to what type of wood to use for the barrels, but all had a gratifying pride in the final result. And the more I looked, the more I shared their appreciation. Their spirits were different, and some of them appealed to me more than others, but each was crafted with such care so that it would be rash to say one was better than another.

As I began to research the book, I found myself getting into the authorial equivalent of method acting: increasingly I wrote myself into the part, appreciating the history, the lore and the present and future of Mexico's gift to the world. I hope this book reflects and spreads my intoxication with the subject.

I

The History and Legend of the Spirit of Mexico

Tequila has only recently entered the Anglosphere, whether as a word or a drink. Earlier in the twentieth century, it was simply one of those exotic drinks, like arrack, ouzo or sake, that intrepid travellers came across during their voyages and wrote about in their tales to shock drinkers who stayed leaning on bars back home. As the century went on, tequila moved into the spirits racks of bars and homes, and now, in the U.S. and increasingly in the rest of the world, it has moved into the shelves of premium drinks that bar-owners monitor closely because of their cost.

Even now, drinkers know little about tequila except that it is indissolubly linked to Mexico. Whiskey or whisky has come a long way from its Irish and Scots origins, spreading with emigrants wherever they could grow enough grain to make it, and being emulated worldwide so that today even India and Japan make credible and creditable varieties. Vodka, Eastern Europe's contribution, is made from almost any organic substance all over the world, just as brandy and rum are made wherever grapes and sugar cane grow. But agave-based spirits, in law, biology and popular consciousness, are as firmly rooted in Mexico's soil as the plants from which they are made.

Pulqueria and *carreta*, Mexico, 1880s–90s.

Unlike the potato, tobacco, cocoa, maize and other New World plants that have conquered the world since Columbus, few other places have the climate for the agave. Potatoes, originally from the Andean mountains in Peru, thrive in Poland to make vodka that the locals consider distinctively Polish, but there are few places that have the long periods of aridity, the volcanic soil and the sunshine that Mexico has; the nation has nurtured over 150 of the 200 varieties of agave in the world.

Even so, mescal and tequila are the product of a similar geohistorical shift and cultural miscegenation. The Poles got their tubers from Peru and distillation from the Arabs, and the Mexican drinks were a product of the convergence of technology that brought gunpowder, the wheel and steel to the New World, as well as the still, which met the endlessly inventive indigenous technologies of making alcohol from agave. Coincidentally they had to meet similar biochemical challenges to the Poles, even though they were hemispheres apart: how to convert the starches of plants like potatoes and the inulin of agaves to sugars, so that the yeasts could work their miracles.

Presumably it helps that there are few other places in the world where farmers have the time and patience to watch a plant grow for a decade or so before it is usable. Along with the geo-biological constraints, that means that the growing worldwide thirst for tequila can only be met from Mexico. The boundaries of climate and altitude are also reinforced by geo-politics – the treaties and conventions protecting tequila and mescal from foreign imitations. Agave can indeed be grown elsewhere, but by law, since 1977 it has not been possible to make tequila outside its national home, and in 1994 the same protection was extended to mescal.

By Mexican law, and international treaties, tequila's national origin is reinforced with strict government regulation that specifies where it can be produced: in the state of Jalisco and specified districts of the states of Nayarit, Guanajuato, Michoacan and Tamaulipas. The largest area for tequila production is in the state of Jalisco, approximately 90 per cent of which has production rights.

Every bottle of tequila displays the number of its distillery (the NOM number). Each distillery is monitored constantly to ensure that they all meet the mandated standards. In fact, tequila production is regulated to the level that each blue agave pod – *Agave tequilana* 'Weber Azul' – is tagged with a GPS co-ordinate and monitored by satellite. The Consejo Regulador del Tequila (or CRT, the official governing entity of the tequila industry) has a laboratory where the DNA of the agave is tested to guarantee its authenticity.

Originally the Spanish conquistadors called the drink that the locals fermented from agave plants *vino de mezcal* – mescal wine. *Mezcal* derives from *metl*, the Nahuatl word for agave, and, some experts add, the word *izcoa*, which referred to the

Regulatory Council testing the product.

fire used to cook the plants, whether for food or brewing. In time people dropped the *vino* and used the name of the plant it was fermented from.

Like many other cultures, the Spanish language in the colonial era did not distinguish between fermented and distilled drinks in the way that English now does. Even now, in many languages like Chinese, 'wine' covers any alcoholic drink, whether distilled or fermented, although in English it only means the latter. *Vino* covered a multitude of ethanol-based sins, and could refer to a drink merely fermented from agave, or one that was distilled from the 'wine'. However, by the end of the nineteenth century, people were only applying the word 'mescal' to the distilled drink, which leads to retrospective confusion now. Add in the change in the meaning of 'mescal' from plant to drink, and mix it with the customary tendency for national and regional pride – not to mention brand marketers – to mythologize ancient histories for spirits, and the result is a cocktail of historical confusion.

Tequila began as *vino mezcal de Tequila*, just a regional variety of mescal named after the town where it was made. Drinkers agreed that the best agave was grown there, in the rich volcanic soil of the mountains, and of course the best spirit was distilled from it. In a region that was often dry, the town had springs that ensured a supply of water for fermenting and later distilling the agave juices. The country itself took its name from one city, Mexico, so perhaps it is not surprising that its iconic beverage is also named after a town. In the Nahuatl language used by the Aztecs, *tequila* means 'the place where you can cut' or 'the place of work', probably because the Tequila volcano's subterranean furnaces produced the black volcanic glass, or obsidian, used to make cutting edges for tools and weapons. The volcano gives the name to the town and to the beverage and the appellation of origin.

But of course the name has spread far beyond municipal, state and even national boundaries. From a parochially regional drink with a localized clientele, tequila is now a major global spirit in its own right, both north of the border in the u.s. and increasingly in the rest of the world. International protection of the protected status of the tequila name is a major goal of Mexican diplomacy. The country's envoys raise the issue in trade negotiations with nations all over the world, and do so with added urgency as tequila's fame and markets spread globally. The name is protected under the North American Free Trade Agreement and in agreements with the eu, and has recently been accepted by Japan. Tequila's product specifications are also registered under wipo – the World International Property Organization.

Until recently you could have said that all agave-based drinks were mescals. Just as cognac or armagnac are brandies from particular regions, so tequila was a mescal from one locality. But if you said that now, you might find lawyers on your case: mescal itself is now also moving upmarket. Instead of being a generic catchall for any spirit made from agave, mescal makers in Oaxaca and the vicinity have turned the name into a regional designation with its own regulatory bodies and intellectual property designation – although using a wider range of agave plants than are found in tequila. Mexican laws to protect mescal have also been adopted by foreign countries.

Even then there are protests that the specifications of how many agave varieties can be used are too restrictive. Following mescal's bid for independence, other regions are building a case that *raicilla*, *sotol*, *sokua*, *bacanora* and other local spirits should enjoy name protection, too. Each of these uses different plants and comes from a different region. *Sotol* (from Chihuahua, Coahuila and Durango states of Mexico) and *bacanora* (from Sonora State) now also have their own appellations of origin.

As we go to print, all of these local spirits are fighting off an empire-building exercise by tequila makers that would restrict their right to use the word 'agave'. Most outside observers think this would probably be a step too far and would certainly meet serious international opposition. It is as if Peru tried to protect the word 'potato', except that that at least is a local term, whereas 'agave' is a classical Latin/Greek name given by a Swede to a plant that grows naturally in places beyond Mexican territory and has been exported to many more.

2
What's in a Name?
Protecting and Branding Tequila

Tequila is not only protected at home and abroad: it is highly regulated, as is mescal, although to a lesser extent. The industry always quotes 'the NOM' but in fact NOM, or Norma Oficial Mexicana, just means 'Official Mexican Standard', of which there are many, each covering different products. However, few of them are evoked as often or as thoroughly as the NOM for tequila, which in full, in its latest manifestation, is known as NOM-006-SCFI-2012, issued in 2012.

The two main bodies of the tequila industry are the Cámara Nacional de la Industria Tequilera (National Chamber of Tequila Makers), which represents the industry and promotes the drink nationally and internationally, and the Consejo Regulador del Tequila (Tequila Regulatory Council) or CRT, which the Chamber founded in 1994. The CRT is a private, not-for-profit organization, but the Mexican federal government has delegated to it the power to monitor and regulate the enforcement of the NOM in the production, bottling and labelling of tequila. The Chamber, representing the overwhelming majority of producers, clearly has considerable influence in determining the specifications for the NOM.

However, once the NOM is decided, the Regulatory Council is robust in its enforcement. Its inspectors continually visit agave fields, distilleries and bottlers to ensure that its mandates are met by producers. It has offices abroad, almost embassies for tequila, in Washington for the USA, Madrid for Europe and Shanghai for China, which monitor the product and aim to prevent counterfeiting. In addition, tequila distilleries maintain their own laboratories to test the sugar levels of the agave, test the wort and the tequila and report that data to the CRT. Many of the larger distilleries host an onsite office for a CRT representative, who is often in almost constant attendance.

The NOM has been amended often over the years, as with, for example, the recent introduction of the 'Extra Añejo' category. In deference to the export markets, it mandates definitions in English as well as in Spanish.

> **Silver** or *Blanco* or *Plata* is unaged, or aged for less than two months. Some tequilas have experimented with bubbling air through it to make it more mellow. The jury is still out on this.
>
> **Gold** or Young, *Oro* or *Joven* is a blend of silver and aged tequila, sometimes with a touch of caramel added for colouring.
>
> **Aged** or *Reposado* is aged in oak containers that must be less than 600 litres in capacity for between two months and eleven months and 30 days.
>
> **Extra-aged** or *Añejo* is aged in oak barrels, again of less than 600 litres, for at least a year, or may be a blend of this and *Extra Añejo*.
>
> **Ultra-aged** or *Extra Añejo* (XO or Extra Old) is aged for at least three years.

The various categories are allowed to vary between 35 and 55 per cent alcohol, although most brands stick to the standard strength for spirits of 40 per cent proof, not least because of

A bottle of Tierras Tequila Blanco.

U.S. regulations, although the majority of brands sold in Mexico itself are 38 per cent alcohol. Makers can add distilled water to bring their product to the desired strength.

Interestingly, in the early days, all tequila had to contain at least 87 per cent of agave-based spirits, but industry pressure and demand from U.S. bottlers led to its dilution: under the NOM, tequila can also be made with up to 49 per cent non-agave-originated alcohols, which are usually but not always based on sugar cane. One well-known brand uses high fructose corn syrup! These tequilas are known in the trade as *mixtos*, but you will not see that description on any bottle. The key detail is that tequilas that do *not* contain other alcohols boast on the bottle that they are '100 per cent agave'. If they do not say that, then they are almost certainly *mixtos*. (In contrast, mescal, which is not bottled in the U.S. and so avoids such lobbying pressures, retains the original proportion of agave in its NOM). Another reason for the practice is that it is difficult for 100 per cent agave products to keep within the methanol limits that some Asian export markets mandate, but *mixtos* can do so.

The CRT ensures that each bottle has a number which identifies the distillery that produced it, even if it is bottled abroad. Under the NOM, 100 per cent agave tequila should be bottled where it is distilled, but *mixto* can be shipped in bulk north of the border to be bottled there, so rail tankers of 110-proof spirit head north all the time. Indeed, not only do they bottle it, but the Americans export it under cover of a wide variety of brands, after which the Mexicans lose track of the market – so global demand beyond the U.S. is probably much higher than the official figures.

In August 2004 the CRT suggested making it mandatory to bottle *mixto* tequila in Mexico, too, in an effort to guarantee the integrity of the drink, which has sometimes been adulterated with other types of alcohol or additives by foreign bottlers. However, distillers were reluctant to invest in additional bottling equipment, and perhaps more decisively, Mexico's NAFTA partners, Canada and the u.s., lobbied hard against the loss of business by their own importers and distributors, and so killed the proposal. While the Mexican government estimates the value of tequila exports to the u.s. was $748 million in 2010, representing a 20.8 per cent growth over 2009, liquor trade figures value global tequila and mescal sales at $2.7 billion in 2009 alone.

Stillmaster Jesús Hernández at work, Olmeca.

Even so, some *mixtos* are premium brands. As stillmaster Jesús Hernández of Pernod Ricard's Olmeca says, 'Some Olmeca varieties include 40 per cent alcohol sourced from the cane sugar and even though sugar is more expensive now, we keep it, because a consistent flavour is very important for a brand.' He concludes, 'You can have a very good *mixto* tequila, and you can have a very bad 100 per cent agave tequila.'

While *mixtos* are permissible, in one respect there is strict alcohol apartheid: tequila producers cannot make mescal, and vice versa.

Global Protection

The National Chamber for the Tequila Industry, which represents the major producers, runs a comprehensive advertising campaign to tell the world's consumers and bartenders about their drink as well as lobbying the government to ensure market access and name protection in foreign countries.

More than the reputations of the companies are at stake. Tequila manufacturers directly employ 30,000 people in agave fields and distilleries and many more in transport and similar industries. It is a significant element in the Mexican economy, all the more so because it cannot be offshored to China, unlike the *maquiladores* on the U.S. border strip, nor overwhelmed by NAFTA competition, as happened to significant sectors of Mexican industry and agriculture.

At the spearhead of the expansion are the *tequileros*, the Mexican makers who, whether employees of multinationals or local families, share an almost religious reverence for the drink and its manufacture.

From Moonshine to Luxury: Branding

Tequila's future, and mescal's, is going upmarket: establishing a perception of quality that allows for a high mark-up and pays dividends in sales revenues. This follows a well-established route for spirits. At one time at the end of the eighteenth century, whisky sales from Scotland to England were curtailed by London, because they competed with the drink of the poor – gin! None of that single-malt, high-end stuff then – elite drinkers sipped brandy or rum.

The growth of interest in premium tequilas has also sometimes been led by relative interlopers, such as Porfidio, Patrón, T1, Milagro and Casa Noble, where devotees have crafted the tequila of their dreams with the hope of capturing a worldwide market. They have carved a niche as boutique luxury brands and have had to build their own distribution networks, bottle by bottle. The major global liquor giants have also moved in and are assiduously promoting their high-end – and high-return – brands, but they generally seem to realize that homogeneity does not work at the luxury end of the market. They know

Varieties of Mexican tequilas, 2010.

better than to impinge on the distinctive identities of the brands while using their worldwide distribution networks to push the product. They maintain the historical haciendas and promote the history and continuity of their brands. Common to all the premium producers is an insistence on quality, which is not to be compromised by bean-counting.

Patrón

John Paul DeJoria started the Patrón Spirits Co. in 1989 with his friend Martin Crowley, an architect who had gone to Mexico for work and brought back an impressive handblown bottle. They saw the potential, added a label and developed the tequila to fill it. John McDonnell, Chief Operating Officer of Patrón International, recalls that 'De Joria was into haircare products so he knew about branding and product placement. Clint Eastwood put Patrón in his movie *In the Line of Fire*, and Wolfgang Puck turned all his friends on to it. Now it is the world's best selling ultra-premium tequila, selling approximately 2,450,000 cases a year.'

Although its tequila is, of course, made in Mexico, the company that owns Patrón is registered in Switzerland. McDonnell adds: 'We're not beholden to shareholders, and every year we've grown, even during the recession, at high prices, and our expansion is self-financed based on private money.' As a result, he explains, 'We do not stint on making it. If the tequila is no good, then no amount of packaging and marketing can make it up – and ours is fantastic. We only use the best agaves, we cook them in clay ovens for 72 hours; we use a *tahona* wheel along with a roller mill.' To leverage an old Western chestnut: there is money in them thar mills. Originally Patrón was made under contract before moving to its own distillery.

Francisco, the stillmaster at Patrón.

Francisco Alcaraz, its veteran stillmaster, explained to me that the distillery is deliberately set up so that even while making large quantities, it is produced in small workshops where the same teams guide each batch through the process. He muses: 'In Germany, our second-biggest market, the biggest brand is a cheaper one, but in London, with its mixology culture, they have really taken up Patrón. All good things take time. We've come from nowhere in a short time.'

Organic Tequila

In 2007 pioneering partners Enrico Caruso and Chris Melendez founded the brand 4 Copas, the first tequila to be certified as organic. Since then health-conscious tequila tipplers have ensured a growing market for it and others like it. Neither the Mexican government nor the CRT specify the conditions for 'organic' tequila, but certainly many common practices, such as adding fertilizers to the mash, would ensure that the resultant spirit would not pass. Generally accepted standards require that organic tequilas are made without pesticides, synthetic fertilizers, sewage sludge, genetically modified organisms or ionizing radiation. It is an uphill struggle, since various pest infestations mean that some agave farmers succumb to the temptation to pump more insecticide onto their fields.

California Certified Organic Farmers (CCOF) and the United States Department of Agriculture both have certifications, but the CCOF is the gold standard, ensuring that the agave is grown organically and that chemical additives are not used in the fermentation and distillation processes. The group even monitors satellite images of the fields to look for signs of chemical use. Conscious of its brand image, Casa Noble, for example, uses the CCOF standard.

However, the need for both good PR and economy have impelled many producers to think of ways to reduce their environmental footprint. The rising cost of energy has led to new attention to ways of reusing the fibres, the *bagasse*, left over after milling – or, in the case of artisanal mescals, from the fermentation. Each litre of tequila generates 5 kg (11 lb) of fibre/pulp solid waste and 10 litres of *vinazas*, the acidic liquid waste left after distillation.

It is indeed a problem, as you can see from the mountains of the stuff near major tequila distilleries, but as the amounts grow it also represents an opportunity. The waste is used as compost or in biogas and paper production, or dried for fuel.

3

Agave: Not a Cactus – But Definitely a Tree of Marvels

Outside my house is a cactus plant
They call the century tree
Only once in a hundred years
It flowers gracefully
And you never know when it will bloom
Victoria Williams, singer, not botanist

One does not want to be too dismissive of plants that can produce such miracles, but grapes are just berries, barley is just a grain and sugar cane is just a grass, and they are all roughly annual crops. However, the plants that make tequila and mescal are a miracle in themselves: the tree of marvels, or *el arbol de las maravillas*, as the conquistadors called the agave plants they watched mature over anything from seven to 40 years.

Agave is the scientific name for the plant the Spanish called *maguey* and the indigenous peoples of Mexico called *mezcal*. They did not pick up the word *maguey* from any of the mainland Mexican languages but from the Carib native peoples, whom the conquistadors had slain and enslaved as they searched in vain for China and gold across the Caribbean before hitting the mainland.

Seedlings of agave.

English-speaking regions call the agave the 'century plant' or the 'century aloe'. Headlines appear regularly in local British and American newspapers when the plants, taken to exotic locations and kept in greenhouses, suddenly come to life and smash through the glass-paned roofs after 40 years or so. A hundred years is a stretch, but a lifespan of 30 years and upwards is entirely common for some types of agave, although, luckily for the economics of the tequila industry, most of the varieties used to make alcohol have shorter reproductive cycles.

The Caribbean islands have their own versions of the plant, but of the 200 or so varieties of agave, most are found in what seems to be their Mexican homeland. Biologists date the genus back 10 million years. It seems to have evolved on the land bridge between North and South America as a specific response to the challenging environment and many microclimates.

In his novel *Mexico*, James Michener called the agave 'a symbol of the Mexican spirit' and waxed poetically but accurately:

> they are like dancers with beautiful hands. They lend grace and dignity to the land and have always been the symbol of peace and construction. From their bruised leaves were made the paper upon which records were kept. Its dried leaves formed the thatch for homes, its fibers, the threads that made clothing possible. Its thorns were the pins and needles while its white roots provided the vegetables for sustenance.

Carl Linnaeus, the Swedish naturalist and taxonomist who developed the whole modern system of classification for plants and animals, gave *maguey* the Greek name 'agave', which meant 'noble, illustrious, or admirable'. He based his typing on exported specimens of *Agave americana*, presumably grown

Agave fields in the native habitat of 'Weber Azul', the valleys near the town and mountain of Tequila.

Mechanization Mexican-style: quick-release panniers for agave *piñas*.

in conservatories in Sweden. The plants impressed European gardeners and botanists with their size and exotic appearance.

The story of the legendary Greek queen Agave, who was indeed a prickly character, might have inspired the name as well. She anticipated future student Spring Break antics under the influence of bad tequila and chemically concocted margaritas. While she and her followers were engaged in ritual binge drinking in honour of Dionysus, she mistook her son Pentheus for a lion. She and her followers dismembered him and carried his head on a stick into town. The myth also prefigures the role of agave-based alcohol for both the sacrificers and sacrificed in pre-conquistador Mexico, which we will deal with later.

Not a Cactus!

Despite the song, 'No, it is not made from cactus' is up there with 'There are no worms in it', as the most frequent correction given to newcomers to tequila. Agaves are easily confused with cacti, since they both evolved to deal with arid and semi-desert conditions, and, like cacti, the visual setting for their juicy greenness is often brown dust.

Agaves and cacti also evolved similar physical defences in order to thrive and reproduce in the face of strong sun, long droughts and hungry animals and insects. Gardeners call both 'succulents' because of the fluid they store in the fleshy interiors beneath their tough outer skins, not to mention the spines that enable them to ward off grazing herbivores. Yet appearances are truly deceptive: the agave is more closely related to onions and asparagus than to cacti. Like them, the agave is in the same plant family as lilies, the Lileaceae, whose members are biochemically imaginative in their defence against insects and similar pests, hence their strong flavours and smells.

Cacti might look odd, but agaves behave even more oddly, like extra-terrestrial infiltrators that break and bend the rules of botany. In their terminal stage agaves look like a cross between a giant pineapple and a man-eating triffid from John Wyndham's science-fiction novel *The Day of the Triffids*. In their relentless versatility and defensiveness, the agave family could well have inspired Wyndham's triffids – and of course their products have been known to lay people low.

For example, as well as a tough cactus-like outer skin that resists water and animals, the agave has more layers of defence. Pest-resistant chemicals in the skin ward off insects, while the sap inside is caustic to many of them. But these rich juices that collect inside see the plant through to its terminal, almost orgasmic growth spurt of flowering and seeding. They are what attract human attention to the plants. Even so, successful *jimadores*, the workers who trim and harvest the *piñas* (hearts) or *cabezas* (cores), carry horns of special cream they have made themselves to protect their hands from these

Trimmed agave.

physical and chemical assaults, which can provoke severe reactions.

The *jimadores* who harvest the agave are a huge reservoir of lore about how to care for the plants and how they should meet their end before being translated into higher things, as it were. Over generations the *jimadores* have developed patterns of planting and distance between plants that avoid the propagation of diseases and tally closely with what botanists and agronomists have calculated, in a more scientific way, delivers the maximum biomass accumulation in this difficult environment. They also choose which of the dozens of varietals are fine-tuned to a local microclimate. They are skilled workers, and the best distillers nurture their teams to preserve that ancestrally acquired expertise.

The piquant chemicals in the skin add zest to the drinks made from them, but it takes refined judgement to calculate how much to use. Too much of the thick skin left on the leaf stumps can make the resulting drink too bitter, and one of the arts of the distiller, in conjunction with the judgement of the *jimadores*, is to judge just how close to the base the *pencas*, the spiny leaves, should be cut. How much is left determines how the strong flavours in the resulting product balance with the distinctive sweetness of the cooked agave.

How the *jimadores* prune the plants, even before harvesting, also varies. For example, near Tequila, the *jimadores* traditionally cut back the leaves with a 'haircut', *el barbeo*, which not only removes the spines at the end of the *pencas*, but concentrates the nutrients in the rest of *piña*. Research has shown that this custom produces larger and more productive pods.

One of the causes for this bio-alchemical broth of juices in the agave is the distinctive, once again almost alien, biology of the plant. Normal earth vegetation transpires through its pores during the day and lets the energy of the sun draw the sap upwards to let chlorophyll do its magic of converting carbon dioxide and water into plant matter. The 'pump' that keeps the circulation going is water evaporating from the leaves and drawing up more from the roots.

In contrast, the agave closes its pores during the day. It acts like a battery, storing up energy from the sun to finish

Well-trimmed agave at Cuervo.

El barbeo (the haircut): cutting back the leaves.

processing it overnight, with what is impressively called the 'crassulacean acid metabolic' or CAM pathway. Instead of converting carbon dioxide and water directly to sugars, the agave makes and stores malic acid at night, when it will lose less water in the process, and waits for the daylight to convert it into nutrients. Malic acid is what gives green apples their tart flavour. Researchers noted that plants that use this process taste bitter in the morning, and it undoubtedly contributes to the distinctive agave taste that tickles the edges of the tongues of tequila and mescal drinkers. It enhances the already very efficient photosynthesis of the plant. The agave is also unique in being the only source of alcohol, perhaps apart from banana beer, that is based neither on sugar nor starch, but on inulin.

It is not only individual plants that have a sturdy survivalist urge. The agave reproduction strategy is not based on the fate of individuals. Rather it is a group response, shuffling the genes to ensure that the agave family as a whole can infiltrate each environmental niche in its geographical range. These plants are swingers, trying out every which way to ensure reproduction. Their capacity to speciate, hybridize and breed new varieties ensures that despite their long lifespan and reproductive cycle, they can colonize all the microclimates – with varied altitude, soil types, water supply, sunshine and seasonal length – with which Central America abounds, straddling the world's two biggest oceans and two continents. The different varieties develop to fit very definite conditions. There is a range of environments that the agave has colonized, but there are limits to it – essentially those found in Mexico at different altitudes. If it gets too cold, or if the temperature rises above 47°C for any time, even the hardy agave gives up. Too much water or bad drainage and some will rot. The *Agave tequilana* 'Weber Azul' legally needed for tequila is adapted to the thin but fertile and well-drained volcanic soils of mountains at altitudes of

An agave literally gone to seed.

between 800 and 1,700 metres (2,000 to 5,000 ft) with annual rainfall of 800–900 mm (315–354 in.) and frost-free temperatures that are preferably around 26°c. That is the ambience of its home in Tequila.

The agave's long life cycle allows it to eke out its water supply over many years to give it time to grow and reproduce. No matter how long it lives, its exotic lifestyle has its penalties – it fruits and then dies. When the agave reaches the botanical equivalent of puberty, from seven years and upwards, the stalk surges from its centre, the *quiote*, shooting up to the height of a tree. There is something Freudian about the tumescent stalk suddenly shooting up to give its seed in a relatively brief burst of passion before the stalk wilts and the plant begins to die.

The locals get the Freudian image, and when they remove it they call it 'castration'. The plants spend all of their resources in that last efflorescence, so the *jimadores* usually castrate it when it begins to shoot. They do not want the juices to go into reproduction, because they want the sugars that would otherwise surge up the *quiote* to remain in the *piña*, the heart, with the nutrients that will make the mescal or tequila.

If the stalk does grow and flower, as it does in the wild, agave sex happens under cover of darkness. Not only does the plant keep its transpiration for night time, but that is when its flowers open to pollination by bats. Sanborn's long-nosed bat (*Leptonycteris sanborni*) feeds on the nectar with a tongue that when engorged is even longer than its nose and thrusts up to a third of its length deep into the flower, exchanging pollen and consummating the match as it does so.

Less than an ounce in weight, the bat is crucial to the agave economy, but it was long millennia before anyone noticed its nocturnal frolicking. There are concerns now that the bat could be an endangered species, not least because so many agave growers cut off the *quiotes* of the hundreds of millions of cultivated agaves before they flower, restricting the bats' food sources. Some farmers now deliberately let a proportion of their plants go to seed to help keep the species thriving.

There is nonetheless a sound reason why those stalks are cut, quite apart from conserving the plant's vital bodily fluids for tequila production. The bats are not picky about where they poke their probosces, so agave varieties mix promiscuously if they are allowed to go to seed. Despite all the scientific rigour associated with the delineation and regulation of the 'Weber Azul' used for tequila, the polyamorous plants hybridize very quickly with natural pollination, so its purity is very precarious.

The unkind cut.

That is why it is rare for tequila producers to use seedlings, since it is unlikely that the offspring would breed true. Mescal makers are more tolerant of variety and several producers are growing agave varieties such as 'Tobala' from seed. The consequences of cross-fertilization were obvious when I visited a farm near Mascota, on the road from Tequila to Puerto Vallarte, where the *Agave maximiliana* variety used for *raicilla* was growing. Each plant had different patterns of leaves and spikes and would probably have been taken for a separate species by the stricter botanists of the tequila industry. But then, to confuse the issue, the plant is also known as *pata de mula* (mule's foot) or *lechuguilla*. Distillers used to harvest it from the wild and it is only recently that farmers have begun to cultivate it to ensure a supply.

Luckily for the botanical purists of the tequila industry, agave doesn't just rely on pollination and seeding. The plants' urge to insure against extinction is so strong that they do not wait until the *quiote* shoots up to reproduce. In fact, when they find a suitable site, they breed like rabbits, an analogy picked upon by Meso-American mythology, whose symbol for the plant was '400 rabbits'. Early in their long life, any time after three years, they put out runners with 'babies', *hijuelos*, that spread from their base. While seedlings have to rely upon the chance of water and suitable weather to take root and grow, *hijuelos* can draw on the nutrients that have been built up in the mother plant through the umbilical cords of the runners. They are effectively clones of the mother plant and are what traditional farmers use to propagate 'Weber Azul'.

Even so, researchers have found that its nocturnal lifestyle, CAM cycle and water efficiency make agave an extremely productive producer of biomass, more so than many other dry-area crops that have been suggested, and far more so than other biofuel feedstocks, such as maize, soybeans, sorghum and wheat. Agave needs no irrigation. E. Garcia-Moya, professor of botany at the Colegio de Postgraduados en Ciencias Agricolas in Texcoco, Mexico, says:

> Agave is a potential candidate as a bio-energy feedstock because it does not compete for land with the production of commodities and it is widely distributed in Mexico. Waste remaining in the fields after harvest, and created during tequila and mescal production, can potentially provide thousands of tons of bioenergy feedstock per year for bioenergy production.

Ana Valenzuela and other researchers have been looking into the possibilities of combining tequila and mescal making with biofuel production. Quite apart from the sugars in the *piñas* and the *pencas*, the *bagasse*, the drained fibres left after milling, can also provide bioenergy production. This would make the Mexican spirits truly global, since shots of tequila would be helping to save the planet – not to mention helping Mexico develop.

Agave Supply

A crop that takes anything from seven years upwards to reach maturity poses problems in the contemporary world of just-in-time supply chains. Sometimes there is a glut of agave and prices become so low that *mixtos* with 49 per cent of other alcohols cost more to produce than the traditionally upper-end 100 per cent agave!

Around the turn of the century, diseases swept the agave terroir and left a shortage, so farmers rushed out to plant in the hope of reaping a big investment. But instead of the usual

After the 'operation' the agave still struggles to reproduce.

A field of 'Weber Azul' agave with Mount Tequila behind.

cycle of renewal, in 2013 their crops were now all reaching fruition together. That contributed to a rush of over 70 new brands of tequila hitting the u.s. market, but it was also storing up problems for the 'Weber Azul' monoculture. Reports suggest that some farmers were simply abandoning their crops, since the prices they could get for them do not make harvesting worthwhile.

Agronomists warn that such abandoned, untended fields of agave can become reservoirs for diseases and pests ready to spread to nearby fields. Major distillers, with an eye to quality control and an assured supply, either grow their own, or contract with farmers to produce for guaranteed prices. That mitigates the cyclical anxieties of disease and oversupply as well as offering the added advantage of assuring the quality and terroir on which premium makers insist.

4
Agave: The Food – and Drink – of the Gods

The Native Americans who travelled down the mountainous spine connecting the North and South American landmasses were quick to appreciate *maguey*'s potential for food in the harsh climate of Mexico. Some tribes still harvest wild agave plants and cook them for food or for fermentation into alcohol. Archaeologists have found evidence of humans cooking and eating agave going back 11,000 years – not long after humans crossed from Asia and populated the Americas. Agave is far more American than apple pie!

It took many generations of domestication to make maize the mainstay of food supply that it became – and it might have been drink rather than food that drove the process. The pioneer alco-archaeologist Patrick McGovern has evidence suggesting that wild precursor of maize, *teosintle*, was actually used to make beer before it was cultivated and bred into maize, suggesting the possibility that it was the urge for alcohol that led to its cultivation and selective breeding. History has always attested to human ingenuity in making food out of any organic product: it is now taking note of even greater ingenuity in fermenting alcoholic beverages out of unlikely feedstock. The Americas are no exception, with ingenious indigenous drinkers making booze with cassava, maize and, of course, agave.

Fire pit for roasting agave on an oak fire.

In contrast to maize, wild agave was just waiting to be eaten. The evidence suggests that it was eaten regularly long before corn, and it seems likely that it was one of the first regularly used plant staples of human life. Archaeologists have been excavating ancient fire pits used to roast the *piñas* from 9000 BCE and in caves they have found preserved quids of chewed fibres and coprolites – fossilized turds – which all show that *maguey* was a significant part of the diet and industry.

But agave is not quite an apple that you can pick off the tree and eat. It needs special and laborious preparation to make it nutritious and even safe before it can be eaten, a process that the plants' size makes more difficult. Across the globe, humans have indeed serendipitously stumbled upon foods that need special treatments to become edible. For example, cassava, the standby for some 500 million people, contains highly poisonous cyanide. It is such an elaborate process to remove it that it almost defies the imagination to see how people persevered in experimentation that must occasionally have been fatal.

Similarly, raw agave has little to commend it as a food apart from its size and seeming lusciousness. Did some proto-Mexican throw agave on the camp-fire to see if it burned? Or did they stumble across accidentally cooked *piñas* caught in a brush fire? It might have been a combination of the two, since Neolithic hunter-gatherers sometimes set bush fires to marshal game into traps, and they would then have been presented with at least one veg to go with their steaks. Indeed the Aztec legend that a lightning bolt hit an agave, cooking and splitting it on the spot, might recall some true serendipitous event – and would certainly suggest divine intervention to the pious or superstitious. No matter who discovered it, roasting *maguey* turns its fairly dull and tasteless inulin into a rich, sweet confection that is full of sugars and many other nutrients. The process is called hydrolysis.

The added advantage of agave is that the whole plant can be used. The leaves provided thatch for roofs, the fibres made rope and fabric, while the spines made needles and the *piñas* gave sugars or 'honey' as well as food. The dried leaves could be used for fuel for cooking, and the leaves made creams

Sandstone ceremonial drinking vessel from pre-Columbian Mexico.

and balms for wounds and burns. There are even depictions of the spiked leaves being used as implements of torture, for example as a penance for priests who neglected their duties!

Pulque

An important part of the agave legend is pulque. Based on Alexander Humboldt's contradictory traveller's account, the myth grew up that tequila and mescal were distilled from pulque, which was never the case. His loose phrasing originated or perpetuated a myth which apparently he also later rebutted, since he distinguished between the agave types used for pulque and those used for mescal. His later self-refutation has not stopped generations of writers from repeating that mescal is distilled pulque. In the town of Comitán in Chiapas they do distil a drink from pulque, but it is so unique that it takes its name from the town – *comiteco*.

In fact pulque is more of a stepmother than a direct ancestor of tequila and mescal, whose heartland was further south and west. While the agave used for tequila and mescal must be

As the 'Codex Mendoza' (*c.* 1540s) shows, in Aztec society the elderly were allowed to drink in moderation. The tipple here is pulque.

roasted and crushed to release the sugars for making alcohol, pulque is the gift that keeps on giving. It is made directly from the sap tapped from the living plant, which begins to ferment naturally. Pulque was drunk around Mexico City and in the heartlands where the half-dozen or so agave varieties that make it flourish.

The original name, *iztac octli*, allegedly meant white wine, but since the pre-Columbian Indians did not have wine, the term is a very loose translation – as in *vino de mezcal*. It's been suggested that the word 'pulque' itself was probably a Spanish mangling of *octli poliuhqui*, which meant 'spoiled wine'.

Aztec nobles and warriors thought it was too good for common people and reserved it for themselves – with some notable exceptions. Pregnant women and the elderly could drink it because of its genuine nutritional qualities. That would scarcely apply to other categories of permitted drinkers – sacrificial victims whose hearts were ripped out by priests who were similarly fortified! Ordinary citizens were allowed to drink it during the five 'dead days' at the end of the year.

Because the plant is tapped instead of being harvested and roasted, pulque is more 'sustainable'. The agave can continue giving for four or five months, and in some cases allegedly for up to three years. But the plant is on borrowed time. Once the *quiote* has begun to grow, the agave is usually on a countdown to demise within a year.

About half a dozen types of agave, such as *Agave atrovirens*, *A. mapisaga* and *A. salmiana*, known collectively as *pulqueros*, are tapped for pulque and many of them are older than 'Weber Azul' when they are ready for harvesting. But not all agaves necessarily produce the stalk, because, in keeping with the reproductive versatility we have already seen, this plant is hermaphroditic. If the *quiote* starts to sprout, it is cut off. The scar is probed repeatedly over some days and its base is hollowed out. The sap that would have surged up the stalk collects instead in the well to give *aguamiel*, honey water. Some of the agave heartlands are so arid that at times of drought the locals drank agave sap instead of water. The *pulqueros* fold the leaves over to cover the scar and the hole in order to protect it between tappings.

Aguamiel begins to ferment naturally even while it is inside the plant. It can be drunk as it is, but when it begins to ferment and bubble it develops a refreshing, tangy taste. People also sell *aguamiel* as a beverage, but if kept too long it is on its way to becoming pulque, which contains between 5 and 8 per cent alcohol, the equivalent of a reasonably strong beer. The traditional way to speed the process of fermentation is to add some already brewed pulque, although sellers often add fruit and other flavourings. An old rumour has it that a sock full of faeces, a *muñeca*, was also used to boost the process, and it is possible that it occasionally was, but it is known that when beer brewers came to Mexico in the nineteenth century they zealously spread the story to kill off the rival product.

As part of the complex of miracles that surround the agave, pulque is almost unique among alcoholic drinks because it does not use yeast to convert sugars into ethanol. The main active ingredient is a bacterium, *Zymomonas mobilis*, but researchers have also found a complex mix of other bacteria and yeasts, including many found in yoghurt production. That seems almost appropriate, since not only does it look milky like yoghurt, but it has tremendous nutritional value. An old Mexican saying is that pulque is *sólo le falta un grado para ser carne* (just a step away from meat). That is probably why the Aztecs allowed pregnant women to imbibe it.

Like yoghurt, pulque often comes with additives mixed in. Fruit and red chilli, Mexican tea, salt, garlic, pepper and anisette are just some of the many flavourings added in various regions

Pulque shop, Tacubaya, Mexico, 1880s–90s.

to its already powerful combination of nutrients, minerals and vitamins.

Cheaper than beer, and usually more potent, it has its own culture, best expressed in the *pulquerias* where it is sold. In traditional places some of its ancient traditions linger in new forms. Women are not allowed into *pulquerias* and traditional makers consider that women's presence during its manufacture will spoil it.

Between the calumnies and seductions of the immigrant beer brewers, and its biologically induced difficulties in commercial distribution and storage, pulque became a downmarket drink and its sales have steadily declined. There have been attempts to can and export it while retaining the biological vivacity that could give it a sales edge in a macrobiotic-inclined world. Once the problem of shelf-life is overcome, it could follow tequila and mescal into the waiting world markets. It does have potential in a health-conscious world as a very nutritious way to get an ethanol fix together with a complex and rewarding mix of nutrients.

It has also recently had a revival domestically, along with all things agave, especially among younger people. 'Pulque is

'Pulque is our weapon in the battle against Neoliberalism!'

our weapon in the battle against Neoliberalism!', a sign on the wall of a *pulqueria* in Guadalajara grandiloquently proclaims.

Pulque, Agave and the Gods

Rabbits, gods, agave and pulque pretty much came as a package in ancient times. In between the proclivities of the Aztecs and other nations for whom pulque was an adjunct to giving heart and soul for deities, the *maguey* and its derivatives also made the pantheon in their own right.

The myths all invoked fertility and fecundity – and thus rabbits! Pre-Columbian peoples used pulque in religious ceremonies for the god Ometotchtli – whose name translates as Two Rabbit. He was just one of the 400 rabbits whose name is now invoked for all tequila drinks. There is no One Rabbit, so there is no deity by that name. Maybe his worshippers only saw double!

With agave's relentless urge to propagate by any means it could, and its ability to survive and provide food and water in the middle of a drought, it is hardly surprising that the peoples of Mexico assumed that it had divine connections. The Olmecs say that a woman, Mayahuetl, discovered *aguamiel* and that her husband Petecatl discovered that it would ferment. For the Nahuatl speakers – the Aztecs – *maguey* had the goddess Mayahuel, who had 400 breasts which each gave pulque.

Another version had Mayahuel chasing rabbits away from her agave plants and discovering one that was wobbling around in circles instead of bounding along in straight lines. She discovered it had been drinking *aguamiel* from an agave, so she and her husband followed the rodent's example – and liked it. And so she should, since one effect was that she became the goddess of *maguey* in its various forms.

In an image from the mid-16th-century 'Codex Magliabechiano', a spider monkey precedes the pulque god.

Mayahuel, goddess of the agave or *maguey*, from the 16th-century 'Codex Laud'.

The Zapotecs, whose descendants now make such good mescal around Oaxaca, relate that Mayatl fell in love with a warrior and produced a wondrous elixir from her breast for him to drink: pulque, of course. The codices in which the survivors and victorious conquerors memorialized the disappearing society contain many depictions of Mayahuel, indicating the affection with which most people regarded her. After all, her worshippers offered up their own livers rather than eviscerated hearts for sacrifice.

Aztec cosmology was complicated – and changeable. In another version, Quetzalcoatl, the white-feathered serpent for whom Cortes was mistaken, fell in love with Mayahuel, a beautiful young maiden who had been entrapped by her evil grandmother. Fleeing the monstrous grandma, he became a willow and she a flowering tree. Her grandmother sent the stars to eat her trunk but when the branches touched the ground they became human remains. Quetzalcoatl lovingly buried them – and they regrew as agave.

Quetzalcoatl, one of the nicest of a fairly ferocious Aztec pantheon, mourned her and the humans who had perished in earlier ages. He had been collecting their bones from the underworld to seed the latest universe. In fact, he was such a sympathetic figure that even the otherwise cruelly demanding gods took pity, and to cheer him up gave him the gift of Centon-Otochli – 400 rabbits, the incarnation of intoxication. The devoted Quetzalcoatl placed it in the core of Mayahuel, the agave, and the rest is bibulous history.

The Bowl of Pulque Game: Tochtecomatl

It's those rabbits again. What seems to be a relatively rare non-lethal game for the Aztecs was Tochtecomatl. The teams of novice priests were summoned by the priest of the god Two Rabbit, and refereed by the priest of Pacetatl. They danced all night around a 'rabbit-bowl' of 'Five Level' pulque – the equivalent of Five Star, set next to the idol of Pacetatl. Five cups were supposed to get the drinker drunk. At the command of the priest, at the end of the night, they rushed to the jar, which had 203 straws placed in it, but in an act of truly Aztec sadism, only one of the straws was perforated. The lucky winner drained the bowl, and the exhausted losers went off to sleep.

5
Mescal Mythology, All Mixed Up?

There are competing versions of the story of how distillation began in Mexico. Either the indigenous nations of Mexico developed distillation before the Conquest, or the Spanish learned it from the Arabs and brought it to the New World, or Filipino coconut cultivators brought in Chinese technology in the late sixteenth century. The final version is that the technology for rum production in the Caribbean flowed across the isthmus.

In the fermentation process, when the alcohol level reaches around 15 per cent, the yeast chokes on its own excretions, and for untold millennia of brewing that percentage was the upper limit. History suggests that if people *can* make stronger booze, they will, but even so it took millennia for the world to move from fermentation to distillation. Traditionally the eureka moment for the technology is thought to have been a combination of Greek and Arab science, derived in part from practical alchemy. Distillation heats the fermented mixture just enough to evaporate the alcohol and then leads it off to condense on a cool surface, leaving behind much of the water. There are likely to have been some martyrs to the gods of booze. Manipulating large amounts of highly flammable vapour next to an open fire is only for the brave, skilled or desperately thirsty, but progress will not be stopped.

The ancient Greek word *ambyx*, transmitted via Arabic with a definite article in front, became 'alembic', and the word is still used for pot stills in Spanish – *alambique*. More recently historians have suggested that China also developed distillation, but the fact that the Japanese word for still, *ranbiki*, comes from the Portuguese word for alembic is indicative that, once exposed to the concept, people took it up with thirsty alacrity.

Alcoholic drinks, and especially branded spirits, accumulate mythology, and not only of the theological kind. Nations want to prove their primacy and claim rights to names – just think of French efforts to secure the sole title to champagne, even before Mexico's diplomatic effort to protect tequila. The historical confusion is compounded because words change their meaning over the years. As we have seen, the meaning of 'mescal' has drifted. At times it meant the agave plant itself, hence *vino de mezcal*, and then occasionally it meant its fermented derivative before coming to mean distilled agave spirits. Now it has been legally redefined to mean only agave spirits distilled in certain districts near Oaxaca.

Mexican national identity and pride is a complex and ever-changing cocktail that incorporates indigenous native Meso-American culture and history with the Creole culture of the Spanish conquistadors who had tried very hard to extirpate that previous culture. Over the years there has been a growing appreciation of the indigenous history and accomplishments, and so it is natural that mescal and tequila, also part of the national identity, should be projected backwards. Proud historians looking back on records referring to *vino de mezcal* assume that it is the modern product, and indeed *tequileros* around the turn of the nineteenth and twentieth centuries called their product *vino de mezcal de Tequila*. But it almost certainly was not what the early Spanish governors of the sixteenth century were taxing in the earliest references to the phrase. Similarly *taberna*

originally meant a tavern, a place where drinks were sold, but by the eighteenth century around Jalisco, it meant a place where *vino de mezcal* was made and sold. By the time the great explorer Alexander Humboldt arrived at the beginning of the nineteenth century, he unequivocally identified mescal as an *aguardiente*, a spirit. But was distillation present before the Conquest?

The present-day artisanal mescal makers in the hills around Oaxaca certainly do not use any technologies or materials that their pre-Conquista Zapotec ancestors could not have used. As we will see later, they still use clay pots for stills and bamboo tubes for worms. Even now, some of them use copper only for the cooling dish at the top, which was well within the reach of pre-Conquest smithing techniques – and indeed in a pinch could also be replaced by ceramics. There have been other suggestions that alcohol could be concentrated by boiling the fermented liquid in ceramic pots and condensing the ethanol in fabric to be wrung out, which could have yielded a stronger drink than just fermented *tepache*. As further evidence, near the volcano of Colima, archaeologists have discovered stone ovens like modern agave pits and decorated funerary vessels with agave images over them – from 1,000 years before the Conquest.

But investigation remains to be done. Drinks leave specific biochemical traces in ceramics and so far no one seems to have tried such tests on the relics. Although agave was treated and fermented, there is insufficient evidence to convince the jury that there was actual distillation.

Bearing in mind the resemblance of the sprouting agave to the triffids in John Wyndham's story, it is something of a coincidence that archaeologists have excavated pots that they label '*Trifid bule, type Capacha*' around the foothills of the volcanoes, and that researchers have actually used the models to make drinkable quantities of mescal, or at least fortified agave alcohol. To be fair the *trifid* refers to the tripod pedestal rather than the anthropophagic plants of the sci-fi story, but archaeologists hypothesize that these were used in religious ceremonies.

Around Colima on the West coast, there are remains that suggest that locals used basic distillation technology without much benefit of metallurgy. One thesis is that Filipinos who had been brought in to cultivate coconut palms in the area imported ceramic Asian stills of the kind they used back home to distil palm wine or coconut liquor, which they called *tuba*. The same name is used even now for local drinks. However,

Venga: the cult of death and mescal march hand in hand.

this could just be an accidental convergence of technology, of the kind that led those who saw Mexican pyramids to decide that they were inspired by their Egyptian and Mesopotamian equivalents instead of the natural constraints of physics and architecture. Certainly there was extensive cultivation of the coconut palm, and wine made from it was, like agave-based drinks, a major source of revenue for the Spanish crown – in between protectionist attempts to ban it.

For example, those ceramic stills, like the Japanese ceramic *ranbiki*, could represent retro-engineering based on seeing 'modern' copper stills at work. Around Colima the Spanish occupation had destroyed the whole demographic and economic base and at various times both agave cultivation and the production of alcohol were prohibited. The native moonshiners had to take to the hills and rely upon appropriate technology with little access to the resources that the cities might have, such as copper and smithing technology, so the primitive techniques might well be imitative adaptions of more modern methods.

Similarly there are reports from the conquistadors of early stills being used to make liquor during the conquest and pacification of Jalisco, based on small alembics, of the kind used by alchemists and apothecaries to make *aqua vitae* for medicinal use. One can presume that battle-weary conquistadors were as broadminded in their use of medicinal spirits as later imbibers, but there are no signs of large-scale commercial production.

While these examples might indeed be testaments to human ingenuity, they are not really part of mainstream mescal and tequila history, even if the eagerness of modern makers to embrace them is eloquent testimony to the patriotic and regional pride in their product.

6

Where It is Made:
The Heart of Tequila

On the far side of Mexico from Spain, local governments more often than not decided that the Spanish brandy whose sales the laws were supposed to be protecting had little marketability anyway. It was a long way from Spain to the mountains and it was more important to raise local funding from alcohol sales, so *vino de mezcal* became a royal monopoly with a 10 per cent excise duty – usually handled by a local agent in an *estanco*, run by local worthies like the Cuervo family in Tequila.

Just as the islands and glens of Scotland are part of the malt-drinking experience, tequila is inextricable from its home region. To an appreciative drinker, savouring a fine liquor is more than the sum of its biochemical constituents and the human palate takes into account more qualities than a gas chromatograph can yield. The history of its home terroir forms an integral part of its aesthetic effect, and there's no terroir like Tequila's!

A few hours north from the evocative colonial centre of Jalisco's capital, Guadalajara, looms Mount Tequila, the impressive extinct volcano that dominates the surrounding plateaux and valleys. A huge cone, often cloud-covered, its peak is despoiled by a radio antenna, which luckily is insignificant against the majestic bulk of the mountain.

Mount Tequila from atop the *Gauchimontones*, a numinous set of cylindrical mounds in the foothills of the mountain.

Nestling on the eastern side is the small town of Tequila, which itself took its name from the mountain and passed it on to the drink. The streams coming down from the mountain cut the steep valleys on the slopes around the town that grow the agave that generations of farmers decided was the best for brewing and distilling – *Agave tequilana* 'Weber Azul' or Blue Weber. Even in the rainy season, the bluish tint of the agaves stands out from the lush green that clothes the slopes, but in the dry season their distinctive colour stands out even more starkly, almost shimmering against the more familiar khaki of sunbaked earth. The whole region is a UNESCO World Heritage site, under UN and government protection, and not just as the birthplace of Tequila and a major tourist destination in its own right.

Some scholars claim that the name derives from the Ticuila tribe, who long ago lived on the side of a volcano. Another

Tequila expert Juan Bernardo Torres Mora gets excited in a field of agave near the town of Tequila.

possible origin is the Nahuatl word *tequitl*, which means work or employment, and the word *tlan*, which means place. The earliest Spanish name for the area was *tequillan*, presumably a phonetic version of the Nahuatl title. So Tequila would be a factory or workshop, and in its way it was a pre-Columbian Pittsburgh or Sheffield: a centre of industry.

Over the hill from the town are the *Guachimontones*, impressively sited sacred mounds. Because ancient architects avoided the sharp angles and edges of other pyramid builders, travellers had assumed the round curves of the mounds to be natural hills. Probing and excavation revealed the complex of stone cones. They seem to be modelled on the cone of Mt Tequila just behind. From the right vantage point, their profiles almost exactly match the volcano silhouetted behind.

From their tips, worshippers could overlook the blue expanse of the lake, which once had floating gardens like those the conquistadors marvelled at in Mexico City. Some of the islands still survive, but are now anchored to the bottom by the tree roots which grew through them to the lakebed below. In the rainy season, their green overgrowth shows the mounds' contours in even more detail. Scattered around the grass and earth one can find the obsidian that raised the place to prosperity in times past. That black glass, smelted in the heart of the volcano, was the sharpest substance in the pre-Iron Age, indeed the pre-Bronze Age before the Conquest. The green lushness of the rainy season, with the underlying stony soil and sharp edges of the obsidian, seems like a physical representation of tequila the drink, vegetal richness laced with a keen cutting edge.

Archaeologists have found postholes on the tops of the mounds and artifacts depicting a man. Was he a priest twirling like a dervish into a trance – doubtless assisted by copious doses of mescal wine? Or was he a sacrificial victim impaled to placate the gods, in which case, once again, his passage

Pyramid shadowed by Mt Tequila. Note how their shapes match.

would have been eased with a cup or two? Among the many violent uses for the obsidian was ripping the hearts out of sacrificial victims, flaying them and similar practices that demanded a sharp edge. However, there is not much evidence that this was done on or near the mounds, despite the regional proclivities for human sacrifice. The complex does include the ball courts, and depending on which version you believe, either the losers were sacrificed or the winners, which would have taken some very sharp refereeing, one imagines. One version has it that the captain of the winning team was offered to the gods, which must have lent a degree of ambivalence to his leadership efforts. Did the team try harder with an unpopular captain?

In the end, when the Spanish came, the locals collectively made the sacrifice, long after the pyramids had fallen into disuse in the ninth century. Coyotl, the king of the region, and his warriors fought long and bitterly against the conquistador Cristobal de Oñate, using weapons made from their local obsidian to great effect. De Oñate was forced to retreat, but with the help of artillery he eventually killed Coyotl, defeated his successor and occupied what became the city of Tequila.

The Town of Tequila

While some historians record the establishment of the town of Tequila in 1531, just a decade after Mexico City fell, it was not until 1650 that Spanish and Indian citizens petitioned the crown to set up a township there, which they fawningly named after the Spanish governor, Torre de Argas de Ulloa y Chavez. Luckily for the town's future drink, they soon dropped this lengthy name in favour of 'Tequila'.

Happily for the conquered, one of the first results of the Spanish Conquest was that the old priestly rules that stopped the laity and commoners drinking pulque evaporated, along with the sacrifices. The historically deprived locals made up for lost time and, as is the nature of the bibulous upper classes everywhere, the hard-drinking Spanish authorities soon began to see drunkenness as a serious problem – where their native subjects were concerned. In particular, landowners accused mine-owners of using agave-based booze to get their peasants drunk so they could shanghai them off the land to work in the mines.

But vying with that censorious attitude was the revenue-raising potential of drinking. Governments want money, and taxing alcohol has always been an easy way to raise it. In most of the French and Spanish colonies, the central government penalized the production of drinks that would rival the home industries back in the metropolis, particularly brandy production. For example, for most of the seventeenth and eighteenth centuries, while the English colonies produced a flood of rum, the Spanish authorities stamped down on its production, even in their own sugar-producing areas.

However, that thirst for cash meant that locally based drink was more often off than on the prohibited list, not least since local cheap booze did not seriously affect the sales of the Spanish wine and brandy industries, whose drinks were prohibitively expensive to transport across an ocean and a continent. Favoured local families, like the Cuervos, based near Tequila, won the state monopoly on production and sale in return for guaranteed revenue for the government.

There are many reasons why *Los Altos* – the highlands – fostered tequila and mescal production. The huge expense of ground transportation across from the Caribbean coast inhibited the import of wines or brandies from Spain, for example, while Madrid's occasional attempts to ban colonial alcohol production encouraged would-be distillers to head for the hills

The oldest tequila distillery: La Rojeña, near the *Guachimontones*.

away from the heavy hand of authority, which, even if it did not ban it, tried to tax it. And of course, some of the best agave grew there.

Mescal itself was made as moonshine for local consumption for much of the period, as Humboldt noticed in his travels in Mexico. However, even when it was sold legitimately it was a more plebeian drink, not one that attracted the upper classes – with the great exception that it was a source of income for the haciendas whose large holdings of land were otherwise not always profitable. Little else would grow but agave in these regions and, as the corn-whiskey makers of Kentucky discovered, distilled spirits had a high value to volume ratio, especially in areas where land transport by wagon or mule train was difficult.

After Mexican independence, far from foreign competition and free of royal interference and taxation, the town and district of Tequila exploited its natural advantages of a good water and agave supply to build up production. This became more and more industrialized as the century went on. By 1888 the city had sixteen *tabernas* distilling the distinctive local product because of the superiority of the local agave from the volcanic soil of the slopes. To the west of the mountain is the even smaller town of Teuchitlán, which houses the picturesque ruins of what some claim is the oldest tequila distillery in the world. The haunting ruins of the hacienda 'La Rojeña' from the nineteenth century are substantially intact – and should be preserved and converted into a museum. Served by an estate of over 5,000 hectares providing the agave feedstock for *vino mezcal de Tequila*, it later lent its name to the Mundo Cuervo distillery.

A German botanist, Franz Weber, who catalogued the agaves with Teutonic attention to taxonomic detail but never saw them in the wild, had sent a French assistant to collect samples and abused his academic privileges by adding his own name. So the local *maguey* became *Agave tequilana* 'Weber Azul' – or Blue Weber. However, it was not the only agave used to make tequila in those days. In the nineteenth century distillers used nine or ten different varieties and researchers like Ana Valenzueala-Zapata have been assiduously tracking them down. She has found mule's foot (*pata de mula*), big hand (*mano larga*), vulture (*zopilote*), *azul listado* and *mezcal chino* all being grown. Some are still used to make mescal, but as we have seen, identifying genuinely distinct varieties from such a polymorphic plant is problematic. Dr Howard Scott Gentry, a revered figure in the small world of agave fanatics, spent a lifetime trying to sort out the taxonomy of the species – but they were probably changing as fast as he categorized them. Like breeds of dogs or cats, it takes a lot of effort to stop them miscegenating and just as a chihuahua can impregnate a pit bull, the different varieties can cross-fertilize.

Bronze agave: modern iconography in the gardens of the Cuervo distillery.

Agave varieties have changed their names over the years as botanists have discovered that the wild and cultivated species are the same, or as similar as makes no difference. *Agave angustifolia* 'Haw' incorporated several varieties, some wild and some cultivated, for example the espadin used to make many mescals near Oaxaca. Even 'Weber Azul' looks different depending where it is grown, with lowland plants producing more oval *piñas* than highland ones, which are rounder. Even the length of the leaves varies with temperature and humidity, and it is possible that a nineteenth-century botanist relying on plant appearances would have identified them as different varieties. But that is one of the secrets of the agave's success: its combination of sexual and asexual propagation make it adaptable to changing threats, whether the climate or pests.

Poring over the leaf shapes and sizes, in 1982 Gentry candidly said of the differences between the espadin and 'Weber Azul' that 'Since these differences are of degree rather than of distinct contrast, their separation as a species is nominal.' He added: 'Certainly the commercial trade with this important economic plant will benefit from the maintenance of this simple binomial', suggesting that there was so much invested in the name and separate identity of *Agave tequilana* that it would be too upsetting to ignore it.

Since 1972, with tightening restrictions from the NOM, and rigorous inspection by the Tequila Regulatory Council, the pressure to exclude all varieties but 'Weber Azul' has grown. No tequila maker would risk 'polluting' the *piñas* with other varieties. The subspecies is now, of course, enshrined as the one and only agave that can be used to make tequila.

Agave Apocalypse: An Endangered Species? Gangrene, AIDS, Drought and Flood

Whether the hills are green during the rainy season, or dry and arid, the slopes around Jalisco are carpeted with the distinctive blue leaves of agave, whose serried ranks march along the contours of the hills. With hundreds of millions of individual plants so visible to all passers-by, it is difficult to think of this feedstock for tequila as an endangered species. But in terms of lack of genetic diversity, that is just what *Agave tequilana* 'Weber Azul' is.

Thanks to the CRT's DNA labs and inspectors, drinkers can be assured that their tipple is made only from 'Weber Azul' and the hundreds of millions of plants that quench the thirst of the distilleries are in effect clones. That purity has its positive and negative sides. To keep within the NOM, the industry can't afford to let them go to seed and cross-fertilize. 'Weber Azul' is like a champion pedigree dog line, so thoroughly genetically groomed that it needs human help to breed true, and maybe even just to survive, as a plant landrace. It has been so intensively farmed that no one has found the original uncultivated rootstock, unlike most other agave types, which also grow wild.

In particular, the memory of the Irish potato famine, in which the one variety grown was devastated by a fungus, haunts agriculturalists, as indeed does reliance on one cloned banana type, the Cavendish, whose world crops have been threatened by disease several times over the years. With little or no variety in the gene pool, diseases and pests could meet little or no resistance and sweep through the agave fields like the Black Death did through Europe.

Over a century ago the plants had already been hit with the 'gangrene of *maguey*', which was only controlled by careful tending. With the exponential growth in demand for tequila – as the agave began to spread on an agribusiness scale, the acreage trebled in ten years – the skills in weeding and tending the plants were diluted, and it is likely that terrains that were only marginally suitable for 'Weber Azul' were brought into cultivation. So in the 1980s similar problems began. Over the years there have been several 'plagues' with colourful names in Spanish – *SIDA del agave tequilero* (Tequila Agave AIDS), *Tristeza y Muerte de Agave* (TMA, The Sadness and Death of the Agave), Agave Gangrene and Red Ring – manifestations of funguses and bacteria-carrying insects such as the agave snout weevil.

Accentuating the problems of pests and pestilence, climate change is another worry for agronomists and environmentalists. Many agave types developed to cope with very precise ecological niches that could change or disappear as temperatures and rainfall change. Agave plants are so finely attuned to their microclimates that they are very susceptible to any change in the climate. Industry veterans still shiver at the effects of a freak snowstorm in the last century.

In any case, the long maturation of the agave leads to economic cycles of boom and bust which amplify the problems. The big companies know the issues. For example, Herradura is exploring how to preserve the integrity of the 'Weber Azul' subspecies while looking for genetic vigour to resist the various plagues that threaten it. During the attack earlier this century which killed off many plants, they took cell cultures from those that survived best and have nurtured them into seedlings in hydroponics from tiny cell cultures, and onto fully grown plants, which they hope will show more resistance while propagating within the limits of the law.

Others insist on rigorously followed planting and harvesting practices to safeguard what is, after all, a long-term investment of labour and capital. No one wants to waste eight years bringing a *piña* to fruition just to see it rot on site. Relying upon the runners reduces the versatility of the overall agave family's defences in the face of environmental changes, climatic or biological. Olmeca's Hernández explained the intricacies of agave selection and nurturing: 'Agave supply is always a big concern of mine. I have an eight-year horizon for my planning so I know how much agave I need to plant every year. We intentionally bring agaves from different areas so that we have diversity.'

He identifies the biggest element as

> how well they're nourished, so if you have a healthy plant they can resist some of the enemies . . . but also the biggest problem that we have with our fields is our neighbors. If you keep your agaves well-maintained and your neighbour doesn't, as soon as you get rid of the pests in your field, you get them from him. Or, if they're not synchronized and you clear the pests in your field and then your neighbor does the same thing at another time, it pushes the pests to your field again. So, we look for new areas to grow our agaves where we don't have neighbours who are agave growers. If they have corn or some other crop, they're completely compatible, but if you have agave next to agave and you don't synchronize the maintenance, you have all kinds of problems.

Controlling all the stages is essential for quality control. Hernández says:

> Now we also control our own distillery. We have our own *jimadores*; we have our own transportation. We harvest only the agave that we're going to load in the ovens every day. So it's on our patio less than 24 hours. It arrives

daily, just in time, freshly cut, and it goes in the oven within 24 hours. It's very important for getting the best of the agave when it's freshly cut. You don't lose sugar. When it dries out, you're losing a lot and that's very important. But before it reaches the distillery patio, the cutting is important. The *penca*, the stub of the leaf has to be about 1 cm, but you can check it visually. There should not be too much green, it has to be primarily white. If the *penca* is already dried out there'll be a dark spot there. If you see too much green on the agave head when it gets here, it's too high. Our three teams of jimadores know exactly what we want.

Originally, they used to have the agave head brought into the distillery intact, 'but that was tougher to load into the truck because it's heavier – up to 40 kilos, and when you unload it, it rolls and it goes everywhere. So we cut them in half in the fields, and we remove the *cogollo*, which is where the leaves meet. If it doesn't have a *quiote*, a flower stem, the *cogollo* is actually bitter and sour even after you cook it, so it can produce flavours in your tequila.'

Once it arrives at the distillery the oven loaders cut the halves yet again, 'using a special very, very sharp axe, so it doesn't get stuck, then they load the agave into ovens in quarters, and they are stacked into the ovens all the way up. Our ovens can hold up to 60 tons of agave each, and it takes a whole three days to cycle. We load; then we steam for about 36 hours; we let it rest and cool down a little bit; then we open the doors, and then we mill it on the third day. We process one oven out of three every day. It goes in cycles.'

The details from large to small are under control. On the small side, he says: 'We have our own yeast strain that we isolated from the agave itself years ago – wild yeast. We experimented with different wild yeasts, industrial yeasts, and we found one wild in the agave that we liked. It gives us the aromas and flavors that we want – a citrus nose, the freshness. And it's also strong enough to be able to process the sugars from the agave at a high concentration.'

A battery of stills at Olmeca.

7
How It is Made:
Do-it-yourself Tequila

Some *tequileros* have a scientific attachment to innovations, experimenting with new techniques at every level from propagation to harvesting, cooking or milling, and right through to distillation. Others have a craftsmanlike attachment to processes that have worked in the past, while some manage to combine the new and old in imaginative ways.

Once they have a product, they want to maintain consistency in case they lose their existing loyal customers. The disaster of the 'New Coke' formula, reviled by everyone outside the Coca-Cola boardroom, haunts all such brand redesigns.

Although the distillers have no leeway in the choice of the type of agave, they can choose their terroir: they can look for volcanic soils, or they can pick terrains closer to sea level. Super-aficionado the Queen of Tequila points out that wine has some 150 identified flavour properties whereas tequila has over 650, and asserts that 'Highland agave often has more fruit and floral notes while lowland agave is often more herbal and spicier.' Of course, highland and lowland are relative terms. Guadalajara is already at an elevation of 1,500 metres (5,000 feet), thus pretty 'high', but the actual highlands, *Los Altos*, and distilleries in Arandas, Atontonilco and Jesus Maria are at 2,000–2,500 metres (7–8,000 feet).

The door of an oven laden with agave ready for cooking at José Cuervo.

Some producers grow their own agave, and some contract with farmers on a long-term basis to buy their product when it is ready for harvesting. Once delivered to the distillery, the agave can meet several fates. More traditional tequila producers cook the *piñas* in clay ovens, usually for 36 hours or more, and let the syrups run off for collection to add to the mash.

Oven doors at Cuervo.

The purpose is to turn the inulin of the agave into sugars that the yeast can work on, to 'hydrolyse the polysaccharides', as chemists put it.

The roasting turns the tough white flesh of the agave a rich caramel colour, making it so tender that strips can be torn off and chewed as a delicacy. Indeed, it is sold as a confection on the streets. Some pressure-cook it in autoclaves, so that it is ready quickly – within four or five hours. This is efficient but frowned upon by traditionalists.

After it is cooked, most makers grind the flesh and extract the sugars in the same way as sugar-cane mills, grinding the pulp between rollers and using hot water to help extract the syrups. These more traditional processes leave behind lots of fibres, the *bagasse*, which is in fact what consumers are left with in their mouth when they chew cooked agave as a candy. The spat-out quids of those fibres found in caves give archaeologists clues about the ancient cooking and consumption of *maguey* millennia ago.

Porfidio seems to be proudly unique in using enzymatic hydrolysis, based on Asian production techniques, to transform the inulin into sugars. Beyond that, instead of cooking and grinding, some producers like Beneva Mezcal or Sauza Tequila use diffusors, which macerate the agave, extract even more sugars from the *piñas* and heat the resulting juices. This is more than looked down upon by traditionalists – it is abhorred. They think it means that the balance of ingredients associated with tequila is lost. Fibre traditionally generates methanol – wood alcohol and diffused tequilas have less of it – which also gives them more access to the Asian markets.

Sauza's publicity claims that 'We mill and steep our agaves prior to cooking the juices to extract the most natural, fresh, crisp agave flavor possible. It's a process we call "Fresh Pressed Agave." It's why margaritas made with Sauza are the freshest tasting.' It's great copywriting, but does not make agave aficionados happy, not least because for *mixtos* they use corn syrup instead of cane sugar.

Purists, who include many drinkers of premium tequilas and mescals, frown upon diffusors, but not so the producers whose sales and margins appear more important – and who doubtless have more clout with the government than those who make and sell the artisanal product. Even so, the cooking methods are different ways to produce the distinctive flavours and aromas needed to build brands.

While tequila producers are more tolerant of new technology, perhaps because their identity is so closely tied to 'Weber Azul', many mescal makers, who use a variety of agave plants, tend to identify their product with the traditional methods used to make it. Doug French of Scorpion Mezcal, for example, joined with some other *mezcaleros* to query the use of diffusors at the organization that controls mescal's Denomination of Origin. However, he reports that the official view was that as long as the modern procedures don't change the taste and quality of the products, then they are acceptable.

French strongly disagrees:

> The diffusor has stripped away the flavor of the mescal and other agave products. I consider their product to be an industrial alcohol made from the agave raw material, not a mescal. I think that those producers should market their product as an agave vodka, not mescal or tequila! So I am disappointed that diffusor production was allowed by the authorities in Mexico.

Ron Cooper, whose Del Maguey brand markets the artisanal mescals that Zapotec Indians make up in their hills with their clay stills, is just as adamant: 'If a producer cooks with steam they should not be allowed to call their product mescal.' For him it is the fire pit and slow distillation that distinguish mescal from tequila.

Fermentation

Once it gets to the fermentation vats, some distillers use commercial yeasts or have isolated their own, such as Herradura, from the local agave. The rationale is that the local yeasts have developed in conjunction with the agave and so are attuned to it.

Commercial yeasts used include wine yeast, bread yeast and even a commercial variety called tequila yeast. One way that distilleries create their own yeast is by perpetual fermentation of their tequila mash in wood vats. Some producers also add fertilizers such as urea to the beer or mash to give the yeasts a boost, but they do not usually advertise that. When

Espadín, a type of agave, in the oven at Scorpion.

the syrup from the ovens is added, that of course enhances the process.

The CRT allows tequila to have 1 per cent additives to enhance the flavour, even when they are certified as 100 per cent agave. Sometimes honey or agave syrup is used to give a sweeter flavour. Mescal does not allow such indulgence.

Traditional artisanal mescal makers ferment in oak tubs, watching for the activity of the bubbles in the fibrous mash. In times past they even used cowhide vats, like pulque makers, and some still claim to. The more industrialized tequila makers put the juices and water in huge stainless-steel vats and let them ferment. It is at this stage that, for the *mixtos*, sugar is added to the brew.

It is an impressive sight to see biochemistry in action, to watch the yeasts begin to work, as the bubbles build up to a frothy head. The *tequileros* monitor the gravity and even the taste of the beer, the mash, to see when they are ready. Once the bubbles stop, that is the time to move the liquid to the still. If

The mashed agave is left to ferment whole for artisanal mescal.

kept open much longer, other micro-organisms will come and convert the alcohol to acetic acid – vinegar.

In some distilleries, in the heat of a Mexican summer, I noticed a phenomenon that was almost a miracle. The workshops are always open-sided, and Herradura is designed so that the surrounding fruit trees and other plants will act as reservoirs for the distinctive mix of yeast fermenting the brew. But there were no flies nor wasps surrounding the vats of sweet sugary mash. They certainly like the cooked agave and cluster around it, so the reason is not any dislike of agave sugars. Herradura suggests that the carbon dioxide and the heavy yeast concentration in the air above the vats might be fatal to the insects. Obviously more research was called for, but tasting the tequila was a more demanding need at the time!

Stills are usually either column stills, named after their Irish inventor Aeneas Coffey, or pot stills, usually known as alembics or *alambiques*. Every distiller has a dilemma. Efficient distillation in column stills produces pure ethanol, pretty much clear, flavourless and aroma-less spirit – vodka, in fact. But customers want tequila, not vodka, so the art of the distiller is to ensure that other compounds from the agave carry over into the condensing chamber, while eliminating the more toxic and noxious ones. Not all those things are good for you! Methanol can make you blind – and can indeed kill those who drink too much of it. Too much methanol, too many aldehydes, fusel oils and other compounds, known as congeners, can give bad tastes or bad hangovers. On the other hand, in the appropriate quantities they are essential to the taste profile that drinkers want and expect.

Pot stills are more expensive to run and take more time but many premium tequila producers prefer them because they often produce a more complex, distinct and flavoursome distillate. Pot stills not only prolong the distillation process,

Fermenting in Tapatío.

remixing volatile compounds that condense before leaving the still, but allow a more complex set of flavours and aromas to condense along with the ethanol. Once distillers have a successful pot still working they are very reluctant to change it, since the shape, composition and other factors all combine in mysterious ways to produce the spirit.

On an industrial scale stainless steel is the material of choice, but it lacks the lustre and allure of copper. Purists prefer copper, which not only conducts heat more efficiently, but, they claim, reacts with sulphur-containing compounds to remove some of the molecules that can contribute overly funky flavours and aromas. Stillmasters even have preferences for different coppers. Some *tequileros* naturally swear by Mexican copper. In addition, things are not always as they seem: some stainless-steel apparatuses have copper linings.

The stillmaster's art is to get Goldilocks proportions in the final spirit: not too bland, not too noxious, but just right – flavoursome and smooth but with a bite. An essential part of the process is to take the first distillation and then to redistil it to produce a purer – but again, not too pure – spirit. Science is brought in to test the results and ensure safety, but the chemistry and physics are merely tools in the hands of the practitioner of an art, a craft.

According to the NOM, tequilas must be distilled at least twice, and some brands go for a third distillation, or a fourth and even fifth, which proponents say makes the tequila smoother. Opponents suggest that it does so by producing what is essentially an agave-based vodka, since these additional distillations will have removed much of what makes an agave-based spirit distinctive.

Ageing and 'Ancient Philosophy'

For generations, ageing has not withered but improved the attractiveness of spirits. The oak barrels used for maturation transmute them, making them richer and smoother. Cognacs depend on judicious balancing of different years and display 'VSOP' and similar non-mathematical descriptions to show their age. But whiskies tend to like rules and age statements. Consumers have a general feeling that older is better.

For years, tequila producers put numbers on their labels which hinted at time spent in barrels. After all, agave-based spirits compete in a global market which values premium rums, whiskies and cognacs for their age. On the face of it, it would be difficult for tequila to compete when until recently its oldest avatar, the *añejos*, were aged for less than two years.

Herradura claims to have been the first brand to age tequila, back in 1974, and the NOM has been adjusted several times over the years to ensure harmony in nomenclature and marketing. Most tequilas are now aged, even if for only for weeks. Until recently, two years was the maximum and then Porfidio introduced *extra añejo* — a designation which was, ironically in view of Porfidio's tussles with the CRT, later added to the NOM. Historically, agave spirits were not usually aged. For example, in Cuervo's plant in tequila town they display the old *damajuanas* or demijohns in which it used to be stored, which were made of glass and stone. The makers were keen to ensure that the valuable alcohol did not evaporate, since one of the costs of ageing spirits is the 10 per cent a year lost to the 'angels' share'.

Faced with snobbish aged-malt drinkers, *tequileros* cannily point out that whiskies are made with barley that at best is just one season from seed, and that even the best cognacs use fresh grapes. In contrast, tequila's agave has been cared for and maintained for eight years before it hits the still. The plant needs to be selected, planted and nurtured through years to maturity before being sacrificed to the fire, mill and still, so it has a fair claim to be already an eight-year-old as soon as it hits the bottom of the bottle.

As connoisseurs drooled over age labels for rums and whiskies that went into the decades, tequilas were in danger of losing the snob wars. But now, premium tequilas are inching year by year up the ageing ladder. With the rapid growth of the market for premium spirits, not to mention their profitability, high-end tequilas are increasingly pushing the outer limits of ageing. For example, Casa Noble's five-year-old *extra-añejo* is on the market and they and others are working on seven-year-olds. Tequilas, like other spirits, benefit from maturation, even for relatively short periods, since it takes some of the harsher edges off the distillate. Unlike some wines and rums, the NOMS for both mescal and tequila specify that wooden casks should be used for ageing and dictates their appropriate capacity, thus averting shortcuts such as dropping oak chips into a stainless-steel vat to mimic the effect of barrel-ageing.

An often overlooked part of the art of distilling fine spirits, ageing depends on acute knowledge of wood and its properties. Distillers did not originally design barrels for maturing or ageing products: they were the shipping containers of the day. One man could move many times his weight by rolling them along the ground, and they could be hoisted and stacked with less fear of breakage than glass or ceramics. Made from oak because of its durability and toughness, these huge casks carried a ton of wine. (The connection between a tun and a ton is not coincidental.)

However, although they might have begun merely as receptacles for transportation, they soon had collateral effects on their contents. Devoted drinkers soon noticed that the casks improved the drinks they contained. Indeed, originally some connoisseurs thought that it was the actual voyage in the ships' holds that worked a sea change on the Madeira wines and rums that circulated in the Atlantic trade. Just as smoking, salting or pickling created pleasant flavours in food as a side-effect of their main purpose, that of preservation, the flavours of drinks were developed because of the containers in which we stored them.

Accepted trade wisdom used to be that anything that spent more than 25 years in a cask would be undrinkable. But miracles happen, and, for example, in 2001 the Macallan's cellarmasters discovered a cask of 53-year-old hiding in the back of the cold and damp Scottish warehouse. They tried it, and lo, it was very, very good. And what's more, collectors were prepared to pay a premium for it (currently $13,000). Appleton has just introduced a 50-year-old at $5,000 a bottle. Island rum producers have introduced a truth-in-labelling law, so that the age on the label must be that of the youngest rum in the bottle. Authenticity costs!

Sea air notwithstanding, our collective palates have become accustomed to the flavours and to the nose that the physics and biochemistry of the oak barrels have lent to their contents over the centuries. However, beyond that, the wood of the barrels is more than just a passive container. It is now an active constituent in creating the drink. 'Brown' spirits like rum and whisk(e)y all begin as relatively clear fluids, more like vodka. It is wood that gives them their colouring, and many of the flavours that we associate with the original material – whether grape, barley, sugar cane or agave – actually come from the wood too. Above all we expect tannins, the oaky taste that makes them special. After all, tannins are called that because they are used to tan leather, which puts the puckering effect they have in our mouths into bitter perspective.

But oaks vary. New American oak has a high tannin count and is rarely used except for bourbon, to which it adds a distinctive taste that is so distinctively oaky that American distillers do not usually age their spirits for anywhere near as long as their Irish or Scotch counterparts. By law they can only be used once for American whiskies. They are then eagerly bought up by rum, Scotch whisky and tequila producers after the bourbon has leached out the strongest elements of the tannins. This allows the casks to be used for the longer ageing periods customary for rum and whisky without making them too 'oaky'.

Before being refilled with tequila, the casks are usually toasted, which means that they are flamed inside to leave a layer of charcoal. That 'cooks' the oak, producing sugars and flavourings and introducing new flavours and aromas to the wood surface, more of which is exposed to the spirit.

However, compared with more robust spirits like rum and whisky, the charred and used bourbon casks' flavour soon overcomes the lightness of the agave's overtones, which is why even the *añejos*, with their couple of years in casks, are juvenile compared with rum, for example, which by law in some countries must be aged for at least two or three years.

There are arguments about whether spirits mature without access to oxygen. My own experiences with old bottled spirits suggest that they do indeed improve over a long period in an anaerobic environment, as the various complex organic chemicals in the spirit react together and the long-chain molecules break down. However, in the early stages the porosity of the casks and access to oxygen is an essential contribution to the process.

Normally, however, oxygen permeates in through the wood and reacts with the sharper components of the spirits, mellowing them even as some of their alcohols osmose through the wood to evaporate into the air outside. Agave

'Condoms' on the tops of the barrels at Olmeca: these are intended to restrict the angels' share.

users follow cognac and other spirits in calling this the 'angels' share'. But it is not only the heavenly choir that gets the benefit. Anyone who enters a spirits warehouse or cellar will testify to the celestial, heady odour of long-term leakage into the air. Technology rears its head again, however: some technologically minded *tequileros* have taken to bubbling air through the spirit in an attempt to get the smoothness of maturation without the wood. Others have taken to enclosing the heads of the casts in airproof covers to reduce the evaporation. That is part of a continuum of years of experimentation, trial and error, to maintain the delicate, almost floral notes of the agave that are all too easily overwhelmed by the strong flavours introduced by the ageing process, but set against that is the smoothness that comes from a well-managed ageing process.

Additionally distillers suggest that unlike whiskies or brandies stored in cool conditions, or even rums often aged in warm but consistent conditions, tequila casks are often aged in warehouses exposed to the vagaries of the Mexican mountain weather, with seasonal variations between winter and summer and even between noonday heat and midnight chill. As the oak shrinks and expands it alternately pulls in and expels the agave, accelerating the wood's contribution to the aroma and savour of the spirit.

In their quest for quality, distillers are also experimenting with the ageing process. Some use barrels made with staves of different woods in the same cask. Others use French or Hungarian oak, which is less astringent than the American varieties, lending a more mellow taste to the tequila. Some use versions of the *solera* method and let the spirit repose for periods in a variety of barrels used for other drinks, port, cognac or red wines, moving it around to achieve the appropriate balance. The challenge is always how to achieve the extra mellowness that ageing the agave brings, and the extra price that comes with it, without losing the 'agavaceousness' that makes tequila a distinct drinking experience.

Despite all this ingenuity, and many fine products, many tequila aficionados prefer the younger, silver tequilas in which they can savour the agave in all its glory. Of course, this harmonizes with the palates of a generation brought up on vodka. But the tastes of many premium spirits drinkers developed on the back of the brown spirits, so this will remain a growing market.

Going for a Bottleful of Dollars: The Drive for Premium

Casa Noble's José Hermosillo, together with several other local families, spent twenty years from buying their initial fields to bringing their product to market and invested heavily in producing a tequila that would appeal specifically to the high-end market. They experimented with different woods for ageing before settling on French oak. Based in a centuries-old distillery near the town of Tequila itself, La Corfida, they have tapped into the tourist market to educate people about what is distinctive in their attractively sited complex. Their latest product is aged for five years, which, he claims, represents the equivalent of fifteen years in other products. 'We grow our agaves in the mountains, to stress them, and they take ten years to be ready', he points out. The fruits of that labour are now available in 23 countries, and he considers its price of $130 a bottle very reasonable, considering all the care and capital invested in it.

The premium brands keep more of the added value inside the country. Jesús Hernández, manager of Pernod Ricard's Olmeca Tequila plant, comments: 'It took some time for a lot

The Tequila tour bus. The town brings in tourists, and sends them away with bottles.

of companies in the tequila business to realise that there's a lot of benefits in making premium tequilas. First of all, you don't have to sell a lot of cases to make good money, so it's better to make quality tequila and get a better margin instead of just continuing to make bulk tequila and ship it to the United States, and bottle it with the Safeway brand.' Ricard built its new distillery in *Los Altos* on a greenfield site, and of course they modelled it on a stately hacienda.

Don't Mess with the CRT: The Porfidio Wars

Tequileros have been involved in Mexico's wars and revolutions for centuries and even in this century were on the front line between the Church-backing Christeros and the anti-clerical government of President Plutarco Elias Calles. But at the end of the twentieth century, Jalisco saw another battle in which some of the old tequila hacienda families waged war against a foreign invader – Porfidio tequila, or Porfidio 100% Agave, as it now calls itself. The conflict began in 1991, when Austrian interloper Martin Grassl became, he claims, the 'first newcomer to the tequila industry in 40 years'.

What made it worse was that not only was he not one of the local *tequilero* dynasties, but he was not even Mexican. In fact, he says wryly, 'I was just another gringo asshole.' Porfidio led the way in ultra-premium tequilas. Grassl, who reinvented himself as Ponciano Porfidio for the enterprise, sold the tequila in an elaborate hand-blown bottle with a colourful glass cactus growing from the base.

Grassl charged premium prices and won many plaudits from aficionados. He claims to have introduced many innovations, from enzymatic hydrolysis to using French oak barrels, that set new standards for premium tequila, but this all led to severe jealousy from the old hacienda don families who had dominated the industry in Jalisco. 'My product tasted better', he claims simply, pointing to the new technologies he had introduced to Mexico.

> That made Mexican *tequileros* who had been in the business for six generations look doubly stupid: it was an offence to Mexican 'pride'. I 'colonized' – in the Mexican interpretation of the term – the country with new production concepts and introduced the tequila industry to the modern age. I didn't invent anything. I simply transferred European knowledge about alcohol production to Mexico. Within exactly ten years, I achieved more in the tequila industry than traditional *tequilero* families in three generations. Porfidio was then the number one exported 100 per cent agave tequila brand. In addition, I was only 29 years

old at that stage. Such circumstances generate envy, common to all humans, not only Mexicans.

The local *tequileros* didn't like it. Another government agency confiscated his production and sued him because the glass cactus he fixed in the base of Porfidio bottles was deemed an insult to Mexican pride. He won in the Mexican Supreme Court, but the affair ended inconclusively. Bottles were burnt in public, and one newspaper drew parallels with the (Austrian) emperor Maximilian, whom the French had tried to foist on Mexico – and who was shot!

In 2001 the CRT alleged that he was selling a product that did not meet the NOM for 100 per cent agave, confiscated all the bottles they could find and put an international arrest warrant out for him with Interpol. Grassl was arrested in Panama in 2003. The authorities in Panama eventually refused to extradite him but kept him in prison while examining the case. He fought the allegations in the Mexican courts, accusing local interests of running a feud against him as an uppity foreigner.

Grassl is now prepared to admit to some degree of maladroitness in his approach. 'I was young, under 30, and recognizably wealthy at the time and I succumbed, to an infantile attitude of cultural insensitivity and arrogance – and nobody likes arrogant and insensible people.' He confesses, 'I am not a good team player, less so on a team which I do not like, such as the tequila cartel – I like doing my own thing.'

The *tequileros* persuaded the president to issue an emergency law banning the use of the phrase '100 per cent blue agave' to describe any product that was not officially tequila. Nonetheless, Porfidio is still made in Jalisco and is still on the market, charging a premium, but does not mention tequila on the label, simply advertising itself as 100 per cent agave and inventing a new category: 'SuperJalisco'. It now has its own dedicated distillery, putting it out of reach of the CRT and the regulatory bodies. However, he does not advertise its whereabouts.

Indeed, as it went from strength to strength in sales, Grassl recounts that the head of the CRT later invited him to let bygones be bygones and rejoin. He guffawed and refused, having won legal cases that entitled him to use the word 'tequila' on his product. He claims, plausibly, that it was probably residual grudges about this old feud that led to the attempt in 2012 to bring the name 'agave' itself under the protection of the NOM 186, which led, of course, to opposition across Mexico, and will almost certainly have been regarded as overreach in the rest of the world.

He reminisces,

When you start a company, you have to somehow count the balance not between the economic interest and the cultural interests. In the first ten years I did a lousy job in balancing my convictions against established cultural traditions, and that certainly led to certain resentment towards Porfidio. Also, what differentiates Porfidio from other foreign-owned brands is that historically we sold 60 per cent of our entire production in Mexico.

The other foreign-owned brands 20 years ago, those were brands which were exclusively exported. And this, of course, it's one story to simply export the brands and another one to have your bottles standing in the bottle shop opposite the house where the traditional monopolists live!

In essence, the Porfidio War was a war to acquire the Porfidio trademarks against my will due to my refusal to sell them, hence a hostile takeover by definition. The CRT and Mexican ministers constituted one instrument in that war, no more, no less.

Patrón, equally a pioneer in premium branding, survived without nearly as many problems – and the differences might be instructive. Grassl points out that 'Patrón adamantly refused to sell in Mexico for 20 years, despite a big demand for their products there. That meant they didn't offend Mexican pride, which in retrospect was a very smart thing to do.'

He adds that neither did Patrón's owner and founder live in Mexico, which made him less susceptible to legal attacks. And while Grassl was a lone Austrian, and living in the country with a Mexican ex-wife made him vulnerable, Patrón was initially capitalized through the Paul Mitchell group, whose owner is among the richest Americans, according to *Fortune* magazine. 'That type of financial position inspires respect from enemies, even from the tequila cartel', Grassl suggests.

He continues that Patrón was also for a time part of the Seagrams group before being sold back to its original owner. Seagrams was politically very strong in Mexico, and Bacardi is now also a major shareowner in Patrón. It not only has considerable clout in Mexico, but awesome lobbying power in Washington. It also helps that the director of Patrón is presently the director of the Distilled Spirits Council of the U.S., the very powerful lobby group of the alcohol industry. Taken together, this all makes Patrón politically unassailable in Mexico from any angle.

'Despite all that, Patrón was viciously attacked in Mexico through the different ministries, same as me, but were better able to defend themselves due to deeper political lobbying pockets', Grassl concludes.

The Tequila Revolution:
Grassl's Guide to Tequinology

When I arrived in 1991, everyone used sugar-cane-style mills. The agave goes into the press, and at the same time you inject hot water. What I introduced was hydraulic presses, as in Europe, which don't need water, and so you do not dilute the aroma of the products.

Usually producers hydrolyse the inulin in agave by cooking it to bring out the sugars. Grassl explains,

In the case of Porfidio, we press the agave juice raw from the plant without any heating process, and then we have introduced something completely new in Mexico – enzymatic hydrolysis. The agave plant is the only one inulin plant that alcohol is made from – usually it is made from plants with starch, or those that have direct sugar content, like grapes. We add special inulin enzymes which transform the raw agave juice into fermentable juice with sugar content . . . [this] also solves one of the biggest, yet least known, problems of tequila, which is that with around 300 milligrams per 100 millilitres, tequila has the highest methanol content among spirits. The agave plant is very similar in consistency to wood, with a high fibre content, which gives the methanol problem. Enzymatic hydrolysis reduces the methanol content to below 100 milligrams, similar to a vodka or whiskey.

This process is sometimes used in Asia to make shoju and sake, overcoming similar problems of how to convert plant material to fermentable sugar. It is also the process that the

Elaborate bottles are part of the charm for mescal in Oaxaca.

iconic Grey Goose brand uses to persuade wheat to ferment to make vodka.

Grassl also introduced new technology to fermentation. He explains, 'Traditionally, in Mexico, the juices were fermented in open tanks, and the temperature was controlled by throwing in blocks of ice to cool down them down. They also used to put urea as a fertilizer in the tanks to accelerate fermentation, making the yeast resistant to temperature variations.' His response was to introduce 'temperature-controlled fermentation tanks, which can actually bring out the true aroma of the agave plants'. Finally, a crucial issue was distillation technology. 'When I came to Mexico in 1991, the distillation technology was some 40 years behind American and European standards, so I introduced the country to more efficient stills than the traditional *alambiques*.' Grassl's drive for quality has had many emulators and his parting words are a reminder for people to keep their noses and tastebuds in training, 'Although people see the NOM as some kind of guarantee of quality, they should remember that it is perfectly possible to make bad tequila or mescal with a NOM number.'

The Bottles

As soon as tequila hit the world market, packaging and branding became extremely important. Tequila and now mescal bottles are triumphs of the designers' and glassmakers' arts. Grassl's Porfidio, with its colourful glass cacti set in the base, provoked feigned outrage from rivals. They had a point about the cactus reinforcing false perceptions about agave but Mexico does, after all, have a few cacti littering its deserts. Patrón set another persistent trend with its signature hand-blown, heavy, square bottles.

More elaborate designs followed, along with labels that often hint at ages and pedigrees that frankly might not stand up to close critical scrutiny. In a market where single malts have been clocking up the years, mysterious numbers have become common on tequila labels too, but they often promise more than they can deliver and are more likely to be dictated by marketing calculations than any calendrical considerations. Similarly the iconography of the labels and surface design will follow marketing whims, emphasizing hacienda Hispano-Mexican culture, Meso-American mythology or smart contemporary themes. But almost certainly they will feature Mexico, the home of tequila and mescal, whose hint of danger will attract drinkers even if it does not always entice tourists.

Many distillers follow the way of the world and outsource bottle production to China, but Patrón, as befits a pioneer, brought its production in-house. Tonala, a village on the outskirts of Guadalajara, is known for artisan glass and produces some of the high-end containers.

8

Who Makes It: The Dynasties

There is a stark contrast between the Zapotec people who make their artisanal mescals in moonshine-style operations in the hills around Oaxaca, and the proud would-be Castilian dons making tequila in their haciendas in Jalisco. Almost like feudal lords, the ranchers ran major agribusiness enterprises in which tequila making played a major role. Some idea of the original development is given by the fact that the same word, *taberna*, is often used interchangeably for the places where the tequila was made and where it was sold. Until the nineteenth century the methods for making mescal and tequila were almost identical – roasting the agave in fire pits and milling it with stone – although haciendas could afford the metallurgy to build more sophisticated stills. The differences between what we now distinguish as tequila and mescal reflect a social divide as well as a geographical and technical one.

In haciendas, economies of scale allowed major commercial development and the nearby sugar mills invited technology transfer. So did necessity: the demands for oak firewood for traditional fire pits raised problems of supply and risked deforestation in the surrounding hills with consequential environmental problems, and so more efficient ovens were demanded. Ovens, mills and large-scale stills offered efficiencies in every sense of the word while a dependent peasant labour force offered significant economies. Coincidentally the clearing of the trees for firewood freed up land for agave planting. The domination of the big dons meant that they could contract with farmers to grow their preferred 'Weber Azul' over the other varieties.

But then the 'gangrene of the blue agave' hit, mowing down the agave fields as the *gusano*, the worm that was later to find a nest at the bottom of a mescal bottle, gnawed its way through the plants. Some accounts claim that the state governor, one of the Cuervo family whose industrial-scale distilling enterprise was encouraging mass agave monoculture, offered 500 gold pesos for anyone who came up with a cure. However, it was no scientific breakthrough that tempered the outbreak, but the empirical experience of the *jimadores* who learnt how to recognize and control infestations by trimming the leaves to stop the *gusanos* gnawing their way to the core.

The tequila families shaped the physical and the social and economic landscape. The often interrelated families that owned them still resonate in the world of tequila. Names like Cuervo, Sauza and Herradura still loom over the industry – and for those who persist in seeing tequila as a recent upstart spirit, these families and their stills can boast a longer pedigree than, for example, many renowned 'historical' Scotch distilleries. And boast they do! The families' pedigrees and chivalric coats of arms, going back to colonial times, adorn their homes, products and histories and they score on both counts since they can claim noble Spanish connections along with impeccable patriotic credentials in independent Mexico.

These families retained their haciendas and distilleries across the region and, despite the various revolutions, they seem to have managed to evade or fight government decrees expropriating the agave-growing land that was the basis of their local standing and prosperity.

The dynasties have been deeply involved in politics, as royal officials, during the war of independence, organizing the defence of the town of Tequila against bandits and, in the case of Herradura's owners, going underground in the religious wars between believers and revolutionary government. And as tequila took off, they became involved in Mexican diplomacy, urging the federal government to defend their traditions against foreign imitations. These influential families have helped ensure that the state and federal governments have been generally solicitous of the welfare of the industry, even beyond its undoubted economic importance to the region and the country.

In recent years, many of them have entered into partnerships with, or even sold their companies to, the small dominant group of multinational drinks corporations such as Brown Forman, Diageo, Pernod Ricard, Remy-Cointreau and most recently Beam, all of whom realized that their premium portfolios were incomplete without tequila brands. Even companies like Bacárdi have ensured that they have a pipeline into the industry.

José Cuervo

The Cuervo dynasty traces its Mexican story back to the seventeenth century when Francisco de Cuervo y Valdes y Suarez landed in New Spain as an army officer. With its governmental connections the Cuervo family acquired land in Jalisco, where the family not only grew agave but cannily had one member heading the Real Estanco de Vino Mezcal, the depot for the royal mescal-wine monopoly in the mid-eighteenth century. The family has been at the core of tequila production ever since, claiming to have made the first *vino de mezcal de Tequila de José Cuervo* in the eighteenth century.

Stills at José Cuervo – all that copper makes a difference.

It has maintained close relations with governments ever since. It is the last of the independent producers, although in late 2012 it was in talks with its international distributor Diageo about complete acquisition for U.S.$3 billion. The talks broke down, and in a sign of the times Diageo stopped its existing distribution deal with Cuervo, wanting to go for the rapidly growing premium end of the market.

Ever since José Sauza broke away from Cuervo to set up his own business, there has always been some friction between his successors and Cuervo, perhaps symbolized by the high stone wall that separates their premises, which are situated next door to each other in downtown Tequila. But like all *tequileros*, they cooperate to protect the name of the product – and their influence in it.

Sauza

Don Cenobio Sauza was a bookkeeper for the Cuervo family enterprise, headed at the time by Don Jose Antonio de Cuervo, where he acquired his expertise in growing and distilling agave. He also set up a transport company to deliver the finished product to the thirsty customers. The business made enough for him to run a *taberna*, or distillery, La Antigua Cruz, first leasing it for three years but then buying it outright.

The distillery displayed the spirituality of the spirits business – it had a cross atop the tall chimney of the plant – but it dropped the old name and was renamed *la Perseverancia*. The company claims to have been first to call the spirit 'tequila' as well as the first to export the drink to the United States – three barrels and six jugs in 1873 through the Paso del Norte, now Ciudad Juarez.

It was also a pioneer in using glass bottles – made in Mexico. The labels celebrated the local roots while illustrating the roots of the drink. '*Vino Tequila Garantizado Puro*' (guaranteed pure Tequila wine), they claimed at the bottom, while describing the plant as '*Fabrica de Vino Mezcal Establecida en Tequila Jal. en 1875*' (Mescal wine factory founded in Tequila Jalisco in 1875). The Sauza family bought and leased many distilleries and haciendas over the region, including some from Cuervo, such as La Chorrera, which had originally been built in 1777 when mescal production was technically illegal. In those days it was easier to distil the agave near where it was grown than carry it in ox-drawn wagons across bad roads.

Sauza's growing empire impelled him to seek recognition abroad and at home, in competitions and expositions from Guadalajara to Chicago, and his cosmopolitan outlook was either inspired or reflected by his marriage to an American. Like his remote contemporary Pyotr Smirnov, who took vodka upmarket by investing in medals and prizes, Sauza pushed the product hard. His *mezcal de Tequila* won the 1892 Chicago World's Fair 'Columbian Exposition Brandy Awards'.

Sauza had initially partnered with the Spanish brandy maker Pedro Domecq in the 1970s and then sold its distillery to Domecq in 1988. Domecq was taken over by British company Allied Lyons, to become Allied Domecq, which Pernod Ricard bought and sold as Sauza to Fortune Brands. That American company has now hived off all its spirits businesses as Beam Inc. However the same distillery kept making Sauza through these corporate vicissitudes, retaining its NOM number 1102. In addition to Sauza, it also makes Hornitos and, using more traditional methods, Tres Generaciones.

Sauza is at the forefront of technology, using diffusors and high fructose corn syrup, which, however, does not endear it to some purists.

Herradura

Herradura uses the horseshoe as its trademark and the dynastic legend claims that the founder Aurelio Lopez was walking in his agave fields when he discovered one glittering in the sun. In much of the world the horseshoe is a symbol of good luck, so he built his distillery on the spot and named it after his lucky find. That was in 1870, and the hacienda, San Jose del Refugio in the tiny village of Amatitan on the outskirts of Tequila, is still the headquarters of the brand.

After a long partnership with Brown Forman, the Kentucky-based corporation that makes Jack Daniels, the company bought out the distillery. Herradura is a 100 per cent agave tequila – a principle firmly laid down by the family in the last century when they refused to countenance *mixto*. The new corporate owners appreciate the mystique of premium brands, even using old-fashioned *tahona*-milled agave for some of their products.

El Refugio, the stately hacienda of Herradura with its library and cool courtyards, is an enclave in the midst of the

Modern *tahona*, or stone milling wheel, at Olmeca. This is a mechanized version, minus the mule.

distillery complex now owned and run by Brown Forman. The old hacienda is a quiet, tree-shaded refuge which functions both as the company's headquarters and the family home.

Herradura combines efficiency with tradition in order to maintain its premium profile internationally. It also makes Mexico's leading domestic seller – Jimador – named after the men who cultivate the agave.

Dynasties Meet Destiny – from the Hacienda to the Boardroom

In the modern era, global demand for tequila began to grow and the companies, even large ones, found that they did not have the capital and networks for worldwide distribution. In common with other spirits, they formed partnerships with or sold themselves to the small core of global liquor giants who could sell their products. The relationships have been different, but they ensure that tequila is reaching all corners of the globalized world. The various houses have come to different accommodations.

Global liquor groups began to have genealogies as complicated as those of the tequila dynasties as they acquired and sold companies and distilleries and were forced by anti-monopoly laws in the u.s., eu and elsewhere to shuffle their decks of brands to avoid anti-competition litigation. They had all acquired one or more tequila brands, whether by outright acquisition or by contracting for distribution rights.

Perhaps despairing of acquisitions of old establishments, Pernod Ricard built its own hacienda and brand from scratch in Arandas in the *Los Altos* region of western-central Mexico. The modern building looks like an old hacienda from the distance. Pernod Ricard's Olmeca range includes Olmeca

Tequilas on sale at Tequila Jalisco, Mexico.

itself, Olmeca Altos and Olmeca Tezon, which are marketed extensively outside the u.s. In the glorious mashup of modern marketing deals, the company has a distribution agreement with Avíon, with which it has entered a joint venture. Avíon has achieved the rare distinction of premium status without even trying to acquire a history. Only a few years old as a brand, it is a signpost to the way in which modern marketing creates a brand, but underpinning it is the quality needed to win tasting medals.

9
The One with the Worms –
Sometimes: Mescal

For those of a literary bent, among the many eminent cantinas of the mescal capital Oaxaca is El Farolito, which inspired novelist Malcolm Lowry as one of the favoured watering spots for his auto-destructive mescal-drinking British consul in *Under the Volcano* (1947). Lowry's chronicle of excessive agave alcohol consumption famously declared that a draught of mescal was 'Like ten yards of barbed-wire fence. It nearly took the top of my head off', and contrasted it with tequila, which had seemingly already achieved a separate and superior status by the 1930s. The ambience of the town remains similar – although the drink quality has improved – and the price has shot up with the quality.

Underdevelopment saved Oaxaca's magnificent colonial centre, the Zocolo, from being overtaken by modern highrise office buildings. In contrast, on the hills overlooking the town looms the huge modernistic white concrete circus tent that houses the Guelaguetza, the massive annual celebration with performances by music and dance troupes from the indigenous villages of the region at the end of every July. The festival began before the Conquest, when the rulers of Oaxaca accepted tribute and sacrifices from defeated tribes in the massive temple complex on nearby Monte Alban, which still dominates the city. The sacrifices have been dropped but the dancing continues, and it is the tourists who bring the tribute now. The Guelaguetza coincides with the rainy season, which gives the region a shimmering emerald tint instead of the usual dusty hue. In the past it regularly rained on the parade, so the venue offers shelter in the storms. But for those who do not want to make the sacrifice of trekking up the hill, the dancers also strut their stuff around the Zocolo, which allows visitors to sit in bars and cafés under the shelter of the colonnades, chomping on *chipalines* or *gusano* snacks – grasshoppers and caterpillars roasted with chilli peppers and salt. Even beer comes with lime and chilli – *michelada* – and of course shots of mescal.

Fortuitously, for the past few years the Guelaguetza has coincided with the International Mescal Fair downtown, giving the opportunity to research all the local traditions at once. The producers at the fair, including Zapotec cooperatives and companies buying village production as well as industrial-scale makers, are all immensely proud of their local drink, which is an important expression of their identity.

In 2011 Mexico produced some 12 million litres of mescal and exported some 7 million litres of it. That is less than a tenth of the amounts of its richer cousin tequila, but *mezcaleros* point out that last year exports were increasing at least four times faster than tequila – and that 80 per cent of the production is small-scale and artisanal. Tequila producers continually fight the popular notion that their product ever contained a worm and try to distinguish it from the mescal that they scorn. Even mescal producers sometimes pretend that the worms were only added for tourists, but distilleries up in the mountains do keep a little pot of them, which they break up and add to their product as they sample it. They do indeed add a distinctive and pleasant taste to the drink.

Two years ago, scientists with a sense of fun wanted to test for DNA signatures in the preserving fluid traditionally used to to keep biological specimens. Their tests on mescal found clear traces of worm DNA in the spirit. In the early days of mescal export some companies also sent sachets of powdered caterpillars to accompany the bottles. The Gusano Rojo brand claims to be the first to have put the worm in the bottle. They used the caterpillars of the *Hypopta agavis* moth, which feed on agave leaves, but seem to be regarded as more of a food source than a pest, since they are roasted and sold as *chinicuiles*.

The other worm in the bottles is a serious pest with an unprepossessing name: the larva of the agave snout weevil. It can cause serious damage to the agave, since infections follow its relentless burrowing. Less flavoursome than the caterpillar and paler in colour, putting it in the bottles seems like fitting revenge for its depredations.

The worm almost epitomizes the social divide between the European ranchers of the north and the indigenous peasants of the south with their reliance on creepy-crawly protein sources. There is a clear class distinction between the ornate and luxurious haciendas of the old time families of Tequila and the mud-walled *palenques* of the Zapotec mescal distillers in the hills around Oaxaca. The social divide has been accentuated, as most of the big tequila producers have now been adopted by huge multinational spirits distributors.

For a century the large haciendas of Jalisco have engaged in industrial and commercial-scale production of the mescal that later was called tequila. Protected by their social and political strength, they could also legalize their own production in a way that the *mezcaleros* could not. In contrast, at times the Oaxacan distillers faced repression by the government and functioned almost as bootleggers as the authorities stamped down on their distillation. Depending on the sources, this was

Worms are for wimps! These scorpions are for the bottles of the brave.

for tax reasons, for health reasons or to stamp out competition for the more politically favoured tequila brands. To some extent making a virtue of necessity, artisanal mescals from single villages have been gaining a niche market and getting high prices north of the border. The growing artisanal mescal market might offer *con gusano* as an option, but it is less and less frequent.

Doug French, the expat American founder of Scorpion Mezcal in Oaxaca, also declares that 'worms are for wimps', and instead puts a scorpion in his bottles. He admits that, unlike the worm, it adds nothing to the flavour, but it does put money into the local economy, since he pays local children to collect them. For the record, dead scorpions en masse have a slightly fishy smell. Premium mescals do not have worms – or even scorpions.

He admits to having a mission. 'Oaxaca is the poorest state in all of Mexico, but it has this natural resource of mescal production, and many different agave varieties. I'm convinced that if the mescal industry matures like the tequila industry, it will change the entire socioeconomic situation of Oaxaca. There are modern, industrial plants, but the real mescal industry is using the same techniques they used hundreds of years ago', he asserts. His distillery yard still features the small pot stills, open-fire ovens and grinders that he began with. However, he realized that to produce the quantities needed for export, more mechanized processes were necessary, so he has added ovens and mechanized mills and other improvised but recognizable industrial-scale machinery.

French is experimenting with different woods for casks while making seven-year-old varietals whose subtlety would be obscured by any such insectoid intrusion. In addition to the common espadin, he is also working on tobala, cirial and other agave bases which do indeed offer different and fascinating flavours and aromas.

That has led to a minor agave agricultural revolution. The cultivation of agave for mescal is a huge source of income for

Splitting espadin, a big agave used for some mescals.

many of the peasants in Oaxaca, so it involves more than symbolism for the 25,000 families in the industry. The cash flows directly into the villages whose environs harbour the *palenques* where they make the mescal, so drinkers can get that extra special warm feeling in their heart as well as their liver for helping lift people from poverty. However, the estimated 700 small distilleries are not equipped to compete on the world market. Even the much larger tequila brands need the international drinks giants to distribute their bottles worldwide. So larger bottlers and distributors, who reap most of the benefits, buy and package the local product, although some villages have formed cooperatives and others have arrangements with overseas distributors to ensure a steady income.

Ron Cooper, the American owner of Del Maguey Single Village mescals, comments: 'Really good producers are beginning to thrive economically due to a huge amount of young, under-40 people all over Mexico, who aren't drinking tequila now but are recognizing and consuming artisanal mescal as "what my ancestors drank!"'

Del Maguey was named Distiller of the Year at the 2011 San Francisco Spirits Festival, an intoxicating tribute to his suppliers, who make their spirit in the hills with clay stills and bamboo tubes.

The Mescal Time Machine:
History in Operation

To see history bubbling, I went into the hills to the village of Santa Catarina de Minas, one of Del Maguey's suppliers, in Oactlan in Oaxaca, to the *palenques*, local distilleries built in huts that are open at the side and dug into the ground. Watching the artisanal mescals being made is like stepping back in

An old millstone or *tahona* that is still in use. The mule was having a siesta.

time. This is, after all, how tequila was also made until the late nineteenth century brought industrial-scale production to the richer haciendas of Jalisco.

The *piñas* are harvested, depending on the species and location, anywhere from seven to fifteen years after planting. There are huge differences in sizes, but although one monster weighed 1,500 lb, a more normal range is from 50 to 400 lb. *Palenqueros* split the *piñas* with axes and then roast them in fire pits whose antecedents archaeologists date back 9,000 years. They are stone-lined in an inverted cone shape, and the makers light a large wood fire in the bottom and cover it with stones usually picked from the riverbed. When the stones are hot enough, they are covered with the *bagasse* – the fibres from previously fermented agave.

The chopped but still substantial agave sections are piled up on that and covered with wet grass mats over which soil or more *bagasse* is piled. After five days, their cooked flesh is rich in sugars with a rich caramel colour – and indeed a caramel taste, with the distinctive smokiness that will lend the eventual mescal some of the finer aspects of a peaty malt whisky.

The more 'automated' palenques use a *tahona*, a rotary stone mill drawn in a circle by a donkey or mule over the cooked *piñas* in a stone pit, as they are shovelled in from the side. Others use a stone trough and crush them manually with a large wooden mallet or pestle. Sometimes it is done in a hollowed-out log – a 'canoe'. Most of the distillers do not add yeast, but rely on the natural airborne yeasts to settle in and set the mixture fermenting when water is added to make the mash. Unlike modern tequila makers, who usually crush the juices and syrups for fermenting, *palenqueros* put the whole porridge-like fibrous mass into the oak vats they usually use. Indeed they shovel the same porridge into the stills.

Unaided by the biochemical paraphernalia of the major distilleries, the locals rely on smell, appearance and experience to know when the mash is ready to distil. With good luck the mixture will have 8 per cent alcohol content when it is ready. But sometimes, for no explicable reason, it just does not happen, some *palenqueros* report, shrugging fatalistically.

Fatalism befits the harassed distiller, bearing in mind the amount of work needed and the uncertainty of success. Between five days of cooking, another five of fermentation and then distillation in relatively small batches, the *palenquero* literally lives on the job, monitoring the progress of each batch as if it were a newborn child. Every one has a platform built into the wall where they can park a mattress and sleep with an eye and a nostril open to check the stages of production.

The raids from the revenue officers and the police over the years have ensured that the technology was not going to be enhanced. Stills are sometimes way off the roads, over rocky fords and up hills. It is that earthy, artisanal quality which attracted sympathetic entrepreneurs like Ron Cooper of Del

Del Maguey, a premium mescal that uses artisanal producers.

Maguey, who offer bottles filled exclusively from each palenque – a 'single mescal' to emulate the single malts of Scotland.

Cooper sees it as cultural reinforcement. 'There is a growing cool group embracing all artisanal spirits and true artisanal mescals are the most authentic of historic artisanal spirits.' The market backs his assessment, since they retail for anything from $34 to $320 a bottle. But it is much cheaper and more fun on site!

Doug French used to buy from artisan distillers, then tried the same process himself before graduating to larger-scale production with a Heath Robinson/Rube Goldberg distillery patched together from redundant textile, sugar milling and soda-bottling plants. He sees premium mescal production as a way out of poverty for the poorest state in Mexico – and of course likes the mescal as well.

A stone trough in which agave is pounded with a mallet before fermentation.

Las perlas, or the pearls (bubbles). The stillmaster sucks up the liquor in a straw and then lets them fall into a dish.

In the Hills with Mexican Mescal Moonshiners

'Shtishbeu!', second-generation Zapotec *palenquero* Luis Carlos said – 'Cheers!' in his native Zapotec dialect – as he gestured towards the gourd he had just passed me. The still-warm mescal had only just trickled from the bamboo tube sticking out from the side of the clay pot still. There was no ice available.

Palenques are like roofed-over dugouts excavated into the hillsides. It could be that this design was originally intended to hide them from the police and revenue officials, but it also has a utilitarian purpose. It shelters the fire under the stills from draughts and winds and allows better control over it. Energy input is fine-tuned by putting more wood into the adobe hearth, or by pulling logs out, as Luis studies the quality of the product dripping from the end of the bamboo tube.

After chopping the espadin agave pods into segments, Luis slow-roasts them in a fire pit for four days, and then pounds them with wooden mallets in a stone trough before fermenting them for over three days in oak vats. He moves the mash from the vats into the pot-still 'when it smells right'. The moist fibrous residue left over is piled through a window outside, but he also uses it to seal any gaps in the clay still and around the rest of the elementary apparatus.

The batch is begun by scooping the mash, which is more like a stringy porridge than a liquid, into the base of the still, the *hoyo*. The clay top is then put on, as is the wooden spade, which collects the mescal that condenses in the underside of the water-filled copper bowl set in the top of the still, and sends it down the attached bamboo outflow. Luis reaches through the window just under the roof to grab handfuls of *bagasse* to pack around the joint between bamboo and still.

At the start of the run, the bamboo tube drips the liquor into a half-gourd. This is the heads, which collects the methanols and similar alcohols as the still gets to the optimum temperature. Once a steady flow begins, the *palenquero* sets glass jars to collect it, taking occasional samples to check the quality.

He pours the heads into a demijohn in the corner. 'To throw away?' I ask, only to be mocked. 'Certainly not! That's the best part, the best flavour', he claims. When no more worthwhile alcohol comes off, the apparatus is disassembled. The remaining *bagasse* is scooped out and thrown through the window to await its fate: it might be used as a sealant, oven insulation, cattle feed or compost as the demand goes.

Then the flagons of *shi-shi* are emptied back in for the second distillation: a delicate process, not least since the stuff is inflammable, indeed explosive. Not one test tube is dirtied in the making of artisanal mescal; it all depends on the nose, palate and eye of the *palenquero*. Luis Carlos supervises the process for days on end from his pallet, set into the side of the dugout. Readiness is determined by the number of bubbles, or 'pearls', that are visible in the gourd.

After the second distillation, Luis declared that the spirit was ready and proved it by sucking it up another bamboo tube and letting it flow back. He invited me to sample it: it was remarkably smooth. As his assistants emptied the still to prepare for the next batch, he reached into a pot with a small handful of pink dried *gusanos*, broke one in half and crumbled it into a small glass of his mescal for me, while chomping on another whole one as a bar snack.

The flagons he uses to collect the distillate are decanted into the large plastic containers that are used to ship it to the Del Maguey bottling plant, into which, he claims, he will also add the heads.

As we mentioned earlier in dealing with the history, there is nothing in the apparatus that was not well within the technological capabilities of his Zapotec ancestors and Pre-Conquista Meso-America.

NOM: Mescal Going Upmarket

French goes beyond the worm in his quest to raise the standards for mescal. He was instrumental in the drive by producers to emulate the tequila makers. They have introduced their own NOM and Council to regulate production standards. Known as the COMERCAM, the Mescal Industry Quality Regulation Council, it successfully introduced the NOM in 2005.

It specifies that mescal must be produced in areas within the states of Durango, Guanajuato, Guerrero, San Luis Potosi, Tamaulipas and Zacatecas and, of course, Oaxaca, which makes 70 per cent of all mescal. Besting tequila, where established interests successfully resisted such a move, mescal has

Clay still for artisanal mescal. Clay and bamboo with a little bit of copper, but a lot of skill.

to be bottled in Mexico and does not allow a *mixto* category. For creams and liqueurs additives are allowed, but the alcohol must all come from agave. The NOM allows two types of mescals: Type 1 is 100 per cent agave sugars and, although not commonly used, Type 2 will allow up to 20 per cent of other sugars, so that producers could make fruit-flavoured mescals. Even pulque has a long tradition of being mixed with fruit, so this could be considered in the historical tradition.

But which agave? In contrast to the tequila monoculture in the north, mescal can use any one of the 28 agave varietals that dot the hillsides. Previously many of the agaves used for mescal grew wild, or only in small patches, but in conjunction with the local university, French and his partners for example have been growing them from seedlings and cultivating them.

The main agave species that Oaxacan distillers use are espadin, tobala, mexicana, cirial and barril, the last being one of my personal favourites.

Mescal comes in three age categories, emulating its northern sibling again:

Joven, young or silver is unaged and clear, although caramel or similar colourings can be added to turn it 'golden'.
Reposado, rested, is aged in oak barrels of no more than 200-litre capacity for between two and twelve months, which adds some colour and, as ageing does, mellows the mescal.
Añejo, aged, is matured in oak for at least twelve months with no upper limit.

Distillers are experimenting with the varieties of mescal, the duration of ageing and the types of wood and are pushing the limits upwards. There is money in premium brands.

Other Agave Spirits

Originally, as we saw, all agave-based spirits were mescal, so when the producers based in Oaxaca won an exclusive NOM, excluding other regional traditions, the latter have been trying to assert themselves. This is partly a matter of local pride and regional identity. But we can also assume a commercial imperative. There are revenues from the growing appreciation for such agave-based exotica at home and abroad – above all to the North, where NAFTA allows easier sales.

Patriotic Mexicans are relishing the drinks produced at home and opening bars that celebrate their heritage. The variety is not necessarily a bad thing, but it can be confusing for consumers – especially those who try to sample them all. However, mescal's 'promotion' to an exclusive category excluded other producers of what used to be considered local varieties of mescal. Makers of *sotol*, *sikua*, *bacanora* or *raicilla* and other agave-based rivals, such as *comiteco*, are working hard to get into the international market, producing new distinct 'appellations'

Clubfoot *raicilla* growing.

and definitions with all the fecundity of the agave plant spinning off new varieties, and of course lobbying the federal government to approve them.

Legally *bacanora* can only be made in the state of Sonora, from Agave Pacifica (sometimes called Yaquiana), In 2010 the producers set up El Consejo Regulacion del Bacanora to regularize and promote production. They have begun exporting to the u.s. and elsewhere, particularly the flavoured versions. Its distillation was illegal until 1992, but since 2000 the federal government has issued it an appelation of origin. Only the spirit from the agave variety grown in the Sonora municipalities of Bacanora, Sahuaripa, Arivechi, Soyopa, San Javier, Cumpas, Moctezuma, San Pedro de la Cueva, Tepache, Divisaderos, Granados, Huásabas, Villa Hidalgo, Bacadéhuachi, Nácori Chico, Huachinera, Villa Pesqueira, Aconchi, San Felipe de Jesús, Huépac, Banámichi, Rayón, Baviácora, Opodepe, Arizpe, Rosario de Tesopaco, Quiriego, Suaqui Grande, Onavas, Yécora, Álamos, San Miguel de Horcasitas, Ures and La Colorada can legally be called *bacanora*.

Made in the state of Chiapas near the town of Comitán from which it takes its name, *comiteco* is unique among the agave spirits since it is distilled from pulque or *aguamiel* rather than from cooked agave. *Pechuga* was originally a mescal made with a chicken breast hanging in the still, but as now made by several distillers such as Real Matlatl, the first run marinates with fruit and spices and the entire mix is run through the still for the second distillation. The chicken breast seems to be optional but it is up to vegetarians to find which brands skip the poultry additive.

Raicilla is produced in the mountains in Jalisco above Puerto Vallarta, on the road from Tequila to the coast. From false etymology – the name means 'little root' – it used to be described as made from the roots of the agave. In fact it is

Raicilla rooting in Mascota.

Clubfoot agave destined for *raicilla*.

made from the full agave, just like all the other varieties. The *raicilla* region of Jalisco includes several towns nestled throughout the coastal strip and the Western Sierra, including the towns of Puerto Vallarta, La Huerta, Mascota, Talpa, Atenguillo, Ayutla, Cuautla, Guachinango Miztlán, Chiquilistlán, El Tuito, Cabo Corrientes, San Sebastian del Oeste and Tomatlán, among others.

Sometimes it is made from *Agave angustifolia*, commonly known as '*Chico Aguiar*' or 'Yellow', but mostly it is *Agave lechuguillaor* (*A. maximiliana*), known locally as *pata de mula* (mule's foot). It is an interesting but flavoursome hybrid that some makers cultivate from seedlings, which naturally tend to wide genetic variation.

Originally *raicilla* was sold as moonshine but is now distilled and sold legally from established distilleries. The Consejo Promotor Mexicano del Raicilla promotes it as 'the grandfather of tequila', and, like most of these varieties, it claims a heritage going back to pre-colonial days. Such claims are not provable, of course, but as well as stoking local pride they are also aimed at the tourists in Puerto Vallarte, who provide a convenient export route.

Sikua is from the state of Michoacan, where the indigenous name for agave is *siku*. The Union of Mezcaleros of Michoacan failed in their attempts over several years to join the DOM for mescal and decided to set up their own DOM, making it perhaps the newest of the agave spirits.

Three states, Chihuahua, Durango and Coahuila, make *sotol* from the *sotol* plant, *Dasylirion Wheeleri*, also known as the desert spoon, which is cultivated from seedlings instead of cuttings. It takes between ten and fifteen years to reach maturity, and only ferments when harvested in winter. Unlike most of its distilled compatriots, *sotol* does not (so far) claim a pre-Hispanic pedigree. In fact it was developed by Vinomex, a company consciously looking for an alternative product beyond the restrictions of tequila-pioneered production in the 1970s. Now of course there is the Consejo Mexicano del Sotol AC, the official Sotol Regulatory Council. Other smaller producers are now striving to follow the requirements of *sotol*'s NOM-159 to ensure their place in the growing markets.

10

Going Global

Mexico survived the 'gringo crash' relatively unscathed, and so did its renowned spirits. Global sales of both mescal and tequila carried on growing even more rapidly during the crisis, but sales of premium brands soared. From 2009 to 2010, in the depths of the recession, sales of the premium tequila category rose by 28 per cent and in 2012 managed a still impressive 22 per cent. In some markets the growth is almost unbelievable – for example 76.7 per cent in Canada. Tequila consumption in the United States increased 45 per cent over the previous five years, so it is no surprise that the Central American nation is waking to the touristic power of tequila and its homeland. After introducing an exotic and dubious upstart into the cocktail cabinets of the world, tequila makers, in conjunction with the Mexican government, have been jointly and severally successful in raising the prestige of the category and their individual brands.

Tequileros take comfort not only from the stunning growth rates in tequila sales, but from its relatively low global penetration, which implies much room for expansion. Even so, tequila now sells to more than 100 countries worldwide. While the u.s. remained a large and growing market, taking 77.6 per cent of exports in 2010, that is a smaller proportion than the previous year, despite impressive annual growth of 9 per cent.

Olmeca tequila: these bottles are bound for Kazakhstan!

The drink and its brands need some explanation for novice customers. A common worry of many of the high-end makers for the markets in the u.s. until recently, and even now in the European Union (eu), is that everything consumers knew about tequila came from their experience of cheaper brands used in binge-drinking.

It is a measure of how recently tequila and mescal hit the bars of Britain that the Weights and Measures Act of 1988 still did not include them in the list of spirits that have to be sold in fixed measures. Since cocktails, 'mixtures of three or more liquids', were excluded from the law as well, the main means of dispensing tequila, margaritas for example, would not have been covered in any case. With the growing popularity of premium tequila, not to mention the 'shot' culture, it might be included in some future version of the Act. However, it is unlikely that the elaborate handblown bottles of premium tequilas would be adaptable to the 'optics' that dispense mass-sale spirits in British pubs. In contrast, the companies are educating international

Tequila Lunazul and a Tequila Sunrise.

connoisseurs to sip it like a fine cognac or single-malt Scotch whisky – and to pay similar prices for the privilege.

Germany is listed as the second-largest export market for tequila, though its producers point out that the drink is often sold on from there across Eastern Europe. Even so, as the market heats up, direct sales from Mexico are becoming more common.

Growth rates have been particularly impressive in the BRIC countries. In 2009–10, premium sales grew by an astonishing 46 per cent in Russia, where the fastest growing segment is newly affluent women wanting to drink something more chic and flavourful than the indigenous vodka. Interestingly Cuervo's Mark Bayardo points out that 'in the Russian market, women on the whole drink three times more tequila than men.'

Patrón's expansion was based on its existing customer base being affluent travellers, and, says CEO McDonnell: 'When they fly into major cities and can't find Patrón, they might try something else and then we could end up losing them, so we made sure that Patrón was available at all the high-class restaurants, bars and hotels.' He adds: 'Our duty-free strategy was different. Duty-free is for luxury and we are a premium white spirit that happens to be a tequila. So we went to the duty-free operators and pointed out that they only offered cheaper tequilas. They accepted the concept and it worked and I would say we're now in 45 of the top 50 airports around the world.'

The BRIC nouveaux riches' seemingly insatiable appetite for global luxury brands clearly helps develop the market for expensive tequilas, but the pot of gold at the end of the worm is undoubtedly Asia. The tequila companies have been selling in Japan and Korea for a long time and are working hard on India and China – the biggest potential markets. Salvador Alvarez, managing director for Casa Herradura, points out that the U.S. accounts for 50 per cent of the global market for tequila and Mexico for 35 per cent, which leaves only 15 per cent for the rest of the world. 'That tells you how much of an opportunity we have. We have an operation in China, which is actually one of our premier operations in Asia, and obviously we're looking at the size of the markets and the opportunities in Asia to drive that going forward.' Despite their jealously maintained differences, the premium brands share high price tags. As Casa Olmeca's Jose Jesús Hernández says, 'You raise the price, you sell more. That's Asia. They like premium. They like buying something expensive.'

The premium tequilas have all that it takes to make a luxury brand – a distinctive locally based product involving a lot of hands-on skilled labour, and a history going back to before the Spanish Conquest. Porfidio was possibly the first tequila brand to concentrate on quality and set standards. While the older *tequileros* are consciously going upmarket to meet those demands, some, like Patrón or Casa Noble, began as avowed prestige brands, and have consciously emphasized their labour-intensive processes. Like all the brands they emphasize their greenness with recycling of glass and wastes. However, the very distinctiveness of tequila-making offers a challenge to entry into the Chinese market. The premium brands, made in pot stills, are more likely to breach Chinese import regulations, since they are more likely to be made from 100 per cent agave in pot stills. As we have seen, that tends to increase the methanol content because of the fibre in the agave. The tequila NOM set by the Mexican government specifies a maximum of three parts per million of methanol – but China still had a limit of two parts. Mexican diplomacy has been spearheading the fight for its national liquor and has succeeded in Japan, China and South Korea.

Olmeca's Jesús Hernández comments, 'It's about balancing the whole tequila body. You want some of the heads and tails – the beginning and end of the distillate – because they give aromas and flavour. If you take too much of the tails out, it would be unbalanced.' Herradura is also wrestling hard with the problem, since they are reluctant to tinker with the manufacturing process of their premium brands to meet the Chinese standard. But those aspirant thirsts of Asia beckon.

The tequila makers have an office in Shanghai to help importers and guide them through the bureaucracy. China originally hesitated to accept tequila as a geographically defined product, and delayed signing an agreement to accept the denomination of origin. *Tequileros* were bracing themselves for a river of counterfeit tequila flowing out of China, but before Chinese entrepreneurs saw their chances and took them, China eventually joined the World Trade Organization and accepted the designation.

So for once in Asia, *tequileros* do not really have a major counterfeiting problem. In addition to bilateral treaties granting tequila its exclusive denomination, the agave is protected by geography. It is very much a native of Mexico and its immediate neighbours. Expensive, exclusive and flavoursome, it is made for the new Asian market.

The thought of billions of Indians and Chinese tipplers knocking back tequila is enough to get everyone out planting agave down near Jalisco. However, there are some roadblocks to entering these markets. Many tequila brands hover close to the permitted methanol levels. Some producers are reformulating to meet the lower standard, but reluctantly so, since premium brands are particularly sedulous concerning their profiles. It was not until the end of 2012 that negotiations and technical refinements brought Casa Noble into China's guidelines, opening up a huge market. It is a measure of the importance that the Mexican government gives tequila that, predictably, the import restrictions on the spirit were top of the agenda when the Chinese president Xi Jinping came to the country in 2013. Beijing promptly lifted the restrictions on imports in the spirit of wooing the U.S.'s southern neighbour.

One cannot help wondering how long it will take for some enterprising mescal maker to add a snake to the bottle for the Chinese market.

Zapotec locals recall their ancestors.

The Spirit of the Future

We have touched upon the science-fictional resemblances of the agave plant and its eccentric reproductive habits, as well as its ability to create sustenance in a desert. With climate change, desertification and growing pressure on food supplies, these anomalies bring the plant, and of course its most prominent derivatives – tequila and mescal – into its own.

Other drinks consume grain or fruit that could otherwise be used for food, allowing odious comparisons between luxury drinks and starving people. Tequila, mescal and agave can sell on sustainability and social consciousness as well as the flavour. The web of legal restrictions on their production ensure that a considerable proportion of the economic benefits of the industry accrue to Mexico and the Mexicans.

Growing worldwide demand for premium products has impelled the makers to use their ingenuity to meet the demands and desires of a huge range of customers, and for once the major multinationals do offer opportunities to local producers who can produce spirits for distribution. It is a huge step in human history from the early Amerindian discovery that roasting agave, whether by lightning strike or fire pit, released nutrition, to the present high-tech production. But those Zapotecs, poking in the embers of the furnace, connect us all to our roots in a way that more complex products would not.

Tequila, mescal and their cognate agave-based spirits not only have a history, but a global future as well, to which we should raise one of the increasingly sophisticated glasses.

Recipes

Cocktails

The traditional, quasi-masochistic ritual for tequila and mescal involved citrus and salt to counter the sharp taste of the agave spirit, but few celebrate this drinking liturgy anymore. The tequila is often much better, for a start. Spring-Breakers will do shots unaccompanied by vitamins or minerals, while connoisseurs will nose and sip their premium tequilas from snifters as if they were fine cognacs or single malts.

But the strongly distinctive taste of both tequila and mescal makes them natural inclusions in cocktails in an age when the art of mixology has come back to life to tickle the palates of a new generation of drinkers. Of all of these, of course, the two classics are the Margarita and the Tequila Sunrise, each of which begs for improvisation and experiment around its main recipe. More sophisticated mixers will take into account the different flavours of the brands, perhaps using mescal in cocktails for additional smokiness. Each recipe calls for adaptation to the contents of the cabinet at the time of mixing!

Margarita

Quite apart from riffs on the basic ingredients, this iconic mix can come straight up, on the rocks or frozen, and each of those variations can have sugar or salt around the rim. Notice that there are only three ingredients. When combined in a judicious and tasteful way, these make a crisp fresh Margarita to suit the most discerning palates. Some people prefer to use a 2:1:1 ratio.

1 ½ oz (45 ml) tequila
½ oz (15 ml) triple sec (Cointreau, Curaçao, Combier
or Grand Marnier, for example)
1 oz (30 ml) fresh lime juice
lime wedge for garnish
salt or sugar to rim the glass (optional)

Be imaginative and creative. Combine ingredients with ice, crushed or cubed to taste, mix in a mixing glass and strain into a pre-chilled cocktail glass rimmed with salt or sugar to taste. Serve with a lime wedge garnish.

Tequila Sunrise

This is the official cocktail of the International Bartenders Association and is a test of skill and patience on the part of the mixologist. In the trade it is known as a 'layered shooter'.

1 ½ oz (45 ml) tequila
3 oz (90 ml) orange juice
½ oz (15 ml) grenadine syrup

or

1 ½ oz (45 ml) tequila
3 oz (90 ml) lime juice and soda
½ oz (15 ml) crème de cassis

Pour the tequila, add the ice and then pour the orange juice into the glass over ice before delicately adding the grenadine, using a spoon against the wall of the glass, so it sinks to the bottom without mixing. Neither shake nor stir!

The Tequini

A Tequini is a Martini made with a tequila base instead of gin or vodka, and so white or silver tequilas are usually used. Because it is relatively unbuffered, mixologists recommend a premium blanco tequila.

2½ oz (75 ml) blanco tequila
½ oz (15 ml) dry vermouth
dash of Angostura bitters
lemon twist or olive for garnish

Pour the tequila, dry vermouth and bitters into a cocktail shaker filled with ice. Shake well (remember 007!). Strain into a chilled cocktail glass. Garnish with an olive or lemon twist.

A Sweet Tequini would substitute a good *reposado* tequila and sweet vermouth.

The Brave Bull

Mixes two of Mexico's homegrown spirits, tequila and Kahlua, and is well within the skill set of even a mediocre mixologist.

2 oz (60 ml) blanco tequila
1 oz (30 ml) Kahlua coffee liqueur

Pour the tequila into an old-fashioned glass with ice cubes. Mix in the Kahlua and swirl the glass gently a few times to lightly mix the ingredients.

Spicy Ginger-Mint Cocktail

9 oz (270 ml) Casa Noble Crystal Tequila
4 12-oz bottles of artisanal ginger ale
12 small fresh mint sprigs
1 lime, cut into 6 thin rounds

Fill four 2-cup glasses (450 ml) with ice. Add 1½ oz (45 ml) tequila to each glass and pour in ginger ale to fill. Garnish each glass with 2 sprigs of mint and a lime slice and serve.

Ginger ale has become a gourmet item, so the mixer can dial up the spiciness by judicious choice of more gingery varieties. This serves six, but if thirsty enough smaller numbers of guests could cope.

Autumn Apple

1 oz (30 ml) *reposado* tequila
1 oz (30 ml) fresh pressed apple juice
1 oz (30 ml) fresh lemon juice
½ oz (15 ml) agave nectar

Combine ingredients into the shaker tin with ice. Shake well. Strain in 12 oz (360 ml) Pilsner glass filled with ice.

El Beso Margarita

2 oz (60 ml) Casa Noble Crystal Tequila
½ oz (15 ml) Licor 43
1 oz (30 ml) lime juice
¾ oz (22 ml) agave nectar
¼ oz (7 ml) squeezed orange

Combine into shaker tin with ice. Shake well. Strain in a 12-oz (360-ml) Pilsner glass filled with ice.

Mescal Passion

1 ½ oz (45 ml) mescal
¾ oz (22 ml) fresh lime juice
3 oz (90 ml) passion fruit purée
3 muddled cucumber slices
1 tsp agave nectar
1 oz (30 ml) House Ginger Beer
1 cucumber slice and a pinch of ground chilli

Put the lime, agave nectar and cucumber slices in a mixing glass, and muddle them, adding the rest of the ingredients, then ice. Shake and strain into a rocks glass filled with ice and garnish with the slice of cucumber and pinch of ground chilli.

Pink Lemonade

1 ½ oz (45 ml) Casa Noble Crystal Tequila
1 oz (30 ml) fresh lime juice
1 oz (30 ml) pomegranate juice
½ oz (15 ml) agave nectar
orange peel for garnish

Combine and shake in a shaker tin with ice and strain into a cocktail glass. Garnish with an orange-peel twig.

Harvest Moon

1 ½ oz (45 ml) Mescal Añejo
1 oz (30 ml) apple liqueur
¼ oz (7 ml) pear juice
dash of fresh lemon juice
splash of egg white
pinch of cinnamon

Add ingredients to a shaker with plenty of ice. Shake vigorously, strain into a cocktail glass and garnish with a thinly sliced pear.

Mexicali Blues
—Josh Wortman, spirits specialist, NYC

1 ½ oz (45 ml) Casa Noble Crystal Tequila
½ oz (15 ml) Art in the Age 'Root' liqueur
½ oz (15 ml) wild blueberry syrup
½ oz (15 ml) fresh lemon juice

Combine and shake in a shaker tin with ice and strain into a cocktail glass with ice.

The Noble Experiment
—Joe Valdovinos, Roxanne's, LA

1 ½ oz (45 ml) Casa Noble Blanco
½ oz (15 ml) Orgeat syrup
½ oz (15 ml) ginger tonic
2 dashes Peychaud's bitters
¾ oz (21 ml) fresh lemon juice

Combine, shake in a shaker tin with ice, and double strain into a frozen coupe glass. Garnish with a skewered Luxardo cherry.

The D.F.

2 oz (60 ml) Casa Noble Añejo
1 oz (30 ml) Carpano vermouth
½ oz (15 ml) cherry juice

Combine and shake in a shaker tin with ice and strain into a cocktail glass. Garnish with lime peel.

Watermelon Martini

1 oz (30 ml) Casa Noble Crystal
2 oz (60 ml) watermelon puree
½ oz (15 ml) agave nectar
juice from half a fresh lime

Combine all ingredients in a shaker tin with ice and shake well. Pour into a Martini glass. Garnish the rim with sea salt.

Elderflower Margarita

1½ oz (45 ml) Casa Noble Crystal
½ oz (15 ml) lime juice
1 oz (30 ml) St Germain
½ oz (15 ml) agave nectar
lime for garnish

Stir all ingredients into a glass with ice and garnish with a twisted lime wheel.

Spicy Watermelon

2 oz (60 ml) Casa Noble Crystal
1½ oz (45 ml) watermelon purée
¾ oz (22 ml) lime juice
¾ oz (22 ml) agave nectar
sparkling mineral water
serrano chilli

In a shaker tin, muddle 1 thin slice of serrano chilli with the watermelon juice and agave nectar, and add the tequila, lime juice and ice. Shake to integrate until chilled. Strain into a glass with ice and top with sparkling water. Garnish with a fresh serrano chilli.

Remember the Alamo

1 oz (30 ml) Casa Noble Añejo
½ oz (15 ml) *joven* (unaged) mescal
¾ oz (22 ml) vermouth
¼ oz (7 ml) maraschino
1 tsp absinthe
orange peel for garnish

Stir all ingredients in a old-fashioned glass with ice until very cold. Strain into a large snifter. Garnish with an orange-peel swirl.

Doctor Jack's Moscow Margarita

Blend the base margarita with a small beetroot, ½ teaspoon of horseradish and ¼ teaspoon of garlic. Shake it like you are standing naked in Red Square. Microstrain. Garnish with the beetroot leaf.

Culinary Recipes

Cooking with tequila or its usually smokier sibling mescal is relatively new. Most people drink it instead. But the Mexican spirits can be used in almost any recipe that uses spirits, although, of course, their distinctive flavour profiles lend themselves to some food groups more than others. Generally the strong albeit sometimes subtle tones of the tequila mean that cooks are sparing with the amounts they use. However, since this is new terrain for cuisine, the addition of agave-based spirits to food allows for experimentation and plaudits for those successful pioneers who have a set of pans and dishes and an array of bottles to try.

White or silver tequilas easily work in place of vodkas, while *reposado* or *añejo* will substitute for the 'brown spirits' such as rum, whiskey or cognac. The Mexican spirits work well with citrus and tropical fruits like mango and papaya and especially of course with the avocado. The strong flavour of the spirits also allows it to pair with herbs like coriander (cilantro) and mint that might overpower a blander profile. And of course, peppers, Mexican style, seem a natural accompaniment.

The flavour and aroma of tequila, and particularly of mescal, lends itself to dishes with ham and bacon, ringing subtle changes on the tastes. Shrimp and ceviche also seem to be well-regarded fields for endeavour.

Avocado, Cucumber and Mescal-soaked Mango Guacamole with Crispy Pork Belly
—from Chef Paul Yellin

½ Scotch bonnet or Habanero pepper – seeded and finely diced
or blended
1 red onion, finely diced
1 seedless cucumber, roughly diced
2 avocados, roughly diced
1 garlic clove, smashed and finely diced
2 mango, skinned and diced
2 firm tomatoes, diced
juice of 2 fresh limes
½ cup (225 ml) mescal añejo
sea salt
fresh ground black pepper
olive oil or pumpkin seed oil
½ bunch coriander, finely chopped – and a bit for garnish
3 cups (675 ml) vegetable oil
thin strips of pork belly, poached in boiling water for 10 mins
then patted dry, deep-fried and salted. Bacon can be substituted
for a quicker, smokier twist
plain (all-purpose flour) to dredge the pork before frying

In a small bowl soak the mango in the tequila. In a larger bowl mix all the ingredients except the pork, which will be fried and added just before serving. Serve with tortilla chips.

Salsa *Borracha* (Drunken Salsa)
—from Demian and LeNell Camacho Santa Ana

4 ancho dried chillies
4 pasilla dried chillies
1 medium white onion
1 large clove of garlic, minced
8 oz (240 ml) freshly squeezed orange juice (approx. 3 oranges)
½ cup (115 ml) 100 per cent agave *reposado* tequila (such as NY International Spirits Competition 2013 medalist Sauza Tres Generaciones)
¼ cup (55 ml) extra virgin olive oil
¼ cup grated Cotija cheese
sea salt
black pepper

Slightly toast the chillies for about 1 minute on each side. With gloves, remove the stems, veins and seeds from the chillies, and tear into small pieces. Brown the onion in same pan, then add the garlic, quickly stirring and removing all from pan so as not to burn the garlic. Add the onions and garlic with the chillies, orange juice, tequila and olive oil to a blender. Purée. Add back to the pan and simmer for 10 minutes to thicken. Add sea salt and freshly ground black pepper to taste. Many folks add the crumbled cheese as a topping to the salsa. We often stir it all together. Serve with chips or tacos, or as a flavouring for red meats.

Some stores in the U.S. sell ancho and pasilla as the same thing. Ancho is really dried poblano. In Mexico, pasilla is usually the dried version of a long, narrow pepper called calavaca. Real Cotija cheese is often hard to find in the U.S., so you can substitute tipo Cotija made elsewhere or use a grated real parmigiano reggiano or other harder, aged, salty cheese.

Glossary and Definitions

Glossary: Talk Agave to Me

In order to appear knowledgeable about tequila and mescal, it is always good to throw in some terminology. Because different regions developed their techniques for distilling and fermenting independently – and many of them were not native Spanish speakers – the words used vary from area to area, just like the names of the *magueys* they use.

Depending on where you are, cultivated agaves are grown in *potreros* (pastures), *campos de agave* (agave fields), *Los Altos* (the Highlands) or *huertas* (groves).

Other common words include:

Acocote: The long-necked gourd used to dip the aguamiel

Aguamiel: The honeywater, the sap from the agave

Apilote: The jug used to collect the aguamiel

Bagasse: The fermentation mash for mescal, or leftover fibres

Barbeo: A barber's trim, pruning the *pencas*

Barranco: Open oven

Cabeza: The core of the plant for tequila or the heads of the distillation

Capada: Castrated – the *quiote* (the flowering stalk or inflorescence of the agave plant) is cut

Chacuaco: The chimney of a distillery around Tequila

Charagua: Aged, sweet pulque with red chilli and toasted corn leaves, drunk as a domestic and ritual beverage from Tlaxcala

Chichihualco: Mescal from the Chichihualco de los Bravos in the state of Guerrero

Chiote/Quiote: The flowering stalk of the agave

Coa: The blade that *jimadores* use to trim the agave

Cogollo: The heart, where the leaves meet

Cola: The tails, the last part of the distillate to come from the still

Corazon: The heart of the distillation, between the heads and tails

Gusano: The gold or red caterpillar that is never put in tequila, but sometimes in mescal. It has been and still is used for food

Hacha: The axe used for splitting the *piñas*

Hijuelos or Ijuelos: 'Pups', the shoots or runners of baby agave

Horno: The traditional oven for roasting agave

Ixtle: The fibre from agave, used for paper, rope and string

Jima: Harvesting, trimming the leaves off the heads

Lechugilla: Mescal made with *lechugilla* (a wild agave). Consumed on special occasions as a traditional beverage in Sonora, Chihuahua and Puebla

Maguey: The colonial name of the agave plant that Spaniards picked up in the Caribbean

Metl: The pre-Hispanic name of agave in Nahuatl

Mezcalero: A mescal maker

Molino: The stone mill wheel used for mescal

Muñeca: The sock filled with faeces allegedly used to boost fermentation in pulque

NOM: Normas Oficiales Mexicanas – the official Mexican Standards of tequila, mescal and some other spirits

Olla: The ceramic/copper still used for mescal

Ordinario: The first run from the still before redistillation

Palenque/Palenquero: A small artisanal distiller(y)

Pechuga: Originally a mescal made with a chicken breast hanging in the still but now with an infusion of fruit and spices added before the second distillation

Penca: The leaf of the agave, cut back before roasting

Piña: The trimmed agave for mescal

Sangrita: Spicy mix of tomato juice, orange juice, chilli powder and other ingredients, used as a chaser or co-sip with tequila or mescal

Shi-shi: The first run from a mescal artisanal still

Shtishbeu!: Cheers! in one Zapotec dialect

Tahona: The stone wheel for agave grinding, sometimes known as *molino Chileno*, the Chilean mill

Tecolio: A pulque with agave worms, used in some traditional festivities and special occasions in the state of Oaxaca

Tepache: The drink that used to be made from roasted agave but is now the wash used for distillation or made from pineapples

Tequilero: A tequila maker

Tina: Wooden fermentation vats

Tinacal: The 'brewery' where the *tinas* are filled

Tlachiquero: The harvester of *aguamiel*

Tobala: A small, wild agave grown in the shade at high altitudes in Oaxaca state, used for making mescal and now being cultivated

Tuxca: A type of mescal from Tuxcacuesco, Jalisco

Vara: Measuring rod. One vara is 0.836 metres or 2.8 feet and the ground around each agave should be kept weeded for one and a half varas

Verde: 'Green': a drink made with aguamiel, mint, lemon and vodka. Served very cold in the state of Tlaxcala

Zotol: A drink made from the lower part of the Zotolero agave in the state of Puebla

Pulque glasses

Tornillo: (screw) 0.125 litre
Catrinas: (dandy girl) 0.25 litre
Chivitos: (little goat) 0.5 litre
Cañones: (cannon) 1 litre
Maceta: (flower pot) 2 litre

NOM Definition

4.34 Tequila

The regional alcoholic beverage obtained by distilling musts, prepared directly and originally from extracted material, in the manufacturing facilities of an Authorized Producer, which must be located in the territory specified in the Declaration, derived from the hearts of tequilana weber blue variety Agave, previously or subsequently hydrolyzed or cooked, and subjected to alcoholic fermentation with cultivated or uncultivated yeasts, wherein said musts may be enhanced and blended together before fermentation with other sugars up to a proportion no greater than 49 per cent of total reducing sugars expressed in units of mass, pursuant to this Official Mexican Standard, and with the understanding that cold mixing is not permitted. Tequila is a liquid that, according to its type, is colorless or colored when aged in oak or Encino oak (holm or holm oak) wood containers, or when mellowed without ageing.

Tequila may be enhanced by the addition of sweeteners, coloring, aromatizers and/or flavorings permitted by the Ministry of Health in order to provide or intensify its color, aroma and/or flavor.

Reference to the term 'Tequila' in this NOM is understood to apply to the two categories indicated in Chapter 5, except for express references to '100 per cent agave' Tequila.

4.34.1 Silver Tequila (Blanco)

A product whose commercial alcohol content must be adjusted by dilution with water.

4.34.2 Gold Tequila (Joven or Oro)

A product that may be enhanced by mellowing and whose commercial alcohol content must be adjusted by dilution with water.

The result of blending silver Tequila with aged and/or extra-aged Tequila is considered gold Tequila.

4.34.3 Aged Tequila (Reposado)

A product which may be enhanced by mellowing, subject to an ageing process of at least two months in direct contact with the wood of oak or Encino oak (holm or holm oak) containers. Its commercial alcohol content must be adjusted by dilution with water, as applicable.

The result of blending aged Tequila with extra-aged Tequila is considered aged Tequila.

4.34.4 Extra-aged Tequila (Añejo)

A product that may be enhanced by mellowing, subject to an ageing process of at least one year in direct contact with the wood of oak (holm or holm oak) or Encino oak containers with a maximum capacity of 600 litres. Its commercial alcohol content must be adjusted by dilution with water.

The result of blending extra-aged Tequila with ultra-aged Tequila is considered extra-aged Tequila.

4.34.5 Ultra-aged Tequila (Extra Añejo)

A product that may be enhanced by mellowing, subject to an ageing process of at least three years, without specifying the ageing time in its label, in direct contact with the wood of oak (holm or holm oak) or Encino oak containers with a maximum capacity of 600 litres. Its commercial alcohol content must be adjusted by dilution water.

5 Classification

5.1 Categories

Tequila is classified in one of the following two categories, based on the percentage of natural Agave sugars used it is production:

5.1.1 '100% agave'

Pursuant to Section 4.34 of this NOM, a product whose fermentation may not be enhanced with sugars other than those obtained from the tequilana weber blue variety Agave grown in the territory specified in the Declaration. For the product to be considered '100% agave' Tequila, it must be bottled in the bottling plant controlled by the Authorized Producer, which must be located within the territory specified in the Declaration.

This product must be labeled using one of the following statements: '100% de agave,' '100% puro de agave,' '100% agave,' or '100% puro agave,' to which the word 'azul' ['blue'] may be added.

5.1.2 'Tequila'

The product defined in paragraph one of Section 4.34 of this NOM whose musts may be enhanced and blended together prior to fermentation with other sugars in a proportion not to exceed 49 per cent of total reducing sugars expressed in units of mass. This maximum enhancement of up to 49 per cent of total reducing sugars expressed in units of mass may not be done with sugars from any species of Agave. The 51 per cent of total reducing sugars expressed in units of mass may only be enhanced with tequilana weber blue variety Agave grown in the territory specified in the Declaration.

This product may be bottled in plants not belonging to an authorized producer under strict compliance by the bottler of the conditions set forth in Section 6.5.4.2 and other applicable provisions of this NOM.

5.2 Classes

5.2.1

Based on the characteristics acquired in processes subsequent to distillation, Tequila is classified as:

Blanco or Plata
Joven or Oro
Reposado
Añejo
Extra Añejo

5.2.2

For the international market, the classifications referenced in the foregoing paragraphs may be replaced by their translations into the applicable language, or by the following:

'Silver' for Blanco or Plata
'Gold' for Joven or Oro
'Aged' for Reposado
'Extra-aged' for Añejo
'Ultra-aged' for Extra Añejo

Tequila Brands: The Good, the Bad and the Ugly

With over a thousand brands on the shelves and more coming out every week, the variety of tequilas gets bewildering. It often seems that every celebrity wants one of their own, and now they are joined by hundreds of mescals, let alone other agave-spirit varieties. Many of them are made to order in distilleries which produce different brands – the zealous can check the NOM number of the distillery on each label to work out the origins. Many are simply bulk-made generic agave spirits bottled and packaged. But the really good ones are made to order.

Some brands have exclusive distribution agreements with multinational spirits corporations, which have been wary of investing in Mexico. Such is the case with Cuervo (which Diageo distributed until 2013) and Cabo Wabo (Campari). Other well-known tequila brands with a multinational face are Sauza (Jim Beam), Herradura (Brown Forman), Cazadores (Bacardi), Olmeca (Pernot Ricard), Patrón (previously Seagrams, now 50 per cent Bacardi), El Tesoro (Jim Beam) and Don Julio (50 per cent Diageo). The big brands usually have a full flight of products that range from basic Spring-Break chug-a-lug to premium tipples, but there are smaller premium brands that are now taking advantage of more sophisticated palates.

There is no arguing about taste, so some brands that would have a connoisseur spitting them out in disgust will still have their aficionados. We have tried to avoid the most obnoxious brands, and tended to go for the 100 per cent agave brands unless there are good reasons to consider *mixtos* – whether because of their quality or their quantity of sales!

In the spirit of the times, there are now organic brands with varying certifications. Some nurture their own agave and others buy in, and some claim to be from the highlands where the more volcanic soil and higher altitude lead to longer maturation and – their makers would claim – a more sophisticated flavour. The world of agave spirits hybridizes with as much fecundity as the plant itself. Brands appear, disappear, change their form and take root in different distilleries. This section lists the websites where the most up-to-date information will be available.

Tequilas

Database of all Distilleries and their Products
www.tequila.net/nom-database.html

Since each bottle has to have the NOM number on its label, this identifies where each brand is made – often in a shared location!

4-Copas
www.4copas.com

1921
www.tequila1921.com

Alderete
www.facebook.com/TequilaAlderete

Arta
www.artatequila.com

Avion
www.tequilaavion.com

Cabo Wabo
www.cabowabo.com

Casa Noble
www.casanoble.com

Cava De Oro
www.yankeebarbareno.com/2013/07/30

Cazadores
www.cazadores.com

Chinaco
www.chinacotequila.com

Don Julio
www.donjulio.com

El Destilador
www.destileriasantalucia.com

Excellia
www.excelliatequila.com

Fortaleza
www.tequilafortaleza.com

Gran Centenario
www.proximospirits.com/centenario-1.html

Herradura
www.herradura.com

El Hornitos
www.hornitostequila.com

El Jimador
www.eljimador.com

José Cuervo
www.cuervo.com

Luna Nueva
www.lunanuevatequila.com

Milagro
www.milagrotequila.com

Montalvo
www.montalvotequila.com

Muerto
www.muertotequila.com

Ocho
www.ochotequila.com

Olmeca
www.olmecatequila.com

Orendain
www.casaorendain.com

Partida
www.partidatequila.com

Patrón
www.patrontequila.com

Porfidio
www.porfidio.ch

Pura Vida
www.puravidatequila.com

Qui
www.quitequila.com

Sauza
www.sauzatequila.com

Siembra Azul
www.siembraazul.com

Siete Leguas
www.tequilasieteleguas.com.mx

Suerte
www.drinksuerte.com

T1
www.t1tequila.com

Tapatio
www.specialitybrands.com/brands/tapatio-tequila

Tres Generaciones
www.tresgeneraciones.com

Mescals

Alipus
www.vinecraft.com/portfolio/alipus-mezcal

Beneva
www.mezcalbeneva.com

El Buho
www.elbuhomezcal.com

De Leyenda
www.mezcalesdeleyenda.com

Del Maguey
www.mezcal.com

Fidencio
www.fidenciomezcal.com

Ilegal
www.ilegalmezcal.com

El Jolgorio
www.agavespirits.com/products-el-jolgorio-mezcal.php

Joya Azul
www.joyasmezcal.com

Montelobos
www.montelobos.com

Pierde Almas
www.pierdealmas.com

Real Matlatl
www.realmatlatl.com

Real Minero
www.realminero.com.mx

Scorpion
www.scorpionmezcal.com

Los Siete Misterios
www.sietemisterios.com/main

Sotol

Don Cuco
www.doncucosotol.com

Hacienda de Chihuahua
www.vinomex.com.mx

Bacanora

Pascola Reposado
www.bacanorapascola.com

Raicilla

La Venenosa
www.facebook.com/pages/la-Venenosa-raicilla

Bibliography

De Barrios, Virginia, *A Guide to Tequila, Mezcal and Pulque*
    (Mexico City, 1980)
Flores-Pérez, Patricia, and Patricia Colunga-Garcíamarín,
    'Distillation in Western Mesoamerica before European
    Contact', *Economic Botany*, LXIII/4 (2009), pp. 413–26
French, Douglas, *The Mezcal Kingdom, History, Laws, Production and
    Cocktails* (Oaxaca, 2010)
Garcia-Maya, E., et al., 'Highlights for *Agave* Productivity', GCB
    Bioenergy, III/I (2011), pp. 4–14
Jose Cuervo, The Oldest Tequila Company in the World: A Family History
    (Mexico City, 2009)
Martinez Limon, Enrique, *Tequila, Tradicion y Destino* (Mexico
    City, 2004)
'Mezcal', *Arte Tradicional de Mexico*, no. 98 (2010)
Mitchell, Timothy, *Intoxicated Identities: Alcohol's Power in Mexican
    Histroy and Culture* (New York, 2004)
Mores-Torra, Juan Bernardo, *El Arte de Conocer, Saborear y
    Admirar Tequila* (Jalisco, 2008), at www.
    consultoresenrentabilidad.com
Petzke Karle, *Tequila: Myth, Magic and Spirited Recipes* (San
    Francisco, CA, 2009)
Roy-Sanchez, Alberto, and Margarita de Orellana, eds, *Tequila:
    A Traditional Art of Mexico* (Washington, DC, 2004)
—, and —, eds, *Guia de Tequila, Artes de Mexico* (Mexico City,
    2007)

Sanchez-Lopez, Alberto, *Oaxaca Tierra de Maguey y Mezcal* (Oaxaca, 2006)

'Tequila', *Arte Tradicional de Mexico*, no. 27 (1999)

Valenzuela-Zapata, Ana G., and Gary Paul Nabhab, *Tequila! A Natural and Cultural History* (Tucson, AZ, 2003)

Vargas-Ponce, Ofelia, Daniel Zizumbo-Villareal and Patricia Colunga-Garciamarin, *In Situ Diversity and Maintenance of Traditional Agave Landraces Used in Spirits Production in West-Central Mexico*, Centro de Investigacion Cientifica de Yucatan

Villalobos Diaz, Dr Jaime Augusto, *Sauza, Lineage and Legend: A Family that Created an Industry for all Times* (Guadalajara, 2007)

Walker, Ann and Larry, *Tequila: The Book* (San Francisco, CA, 1994)

Websites and Associations

The Tequila Regulatory Council/Consejo Regulador de Tequila
www.crt.org.mx

National Chamber of the Tequila Industry (CNIT)/La Cámara
Nacional de la Industria Tequilera
www.tequileros.org

The Tequila Society UK
www.thetequilasociety.co.uk

European Tequila Aficionado site
www.tequilaland.de

Tequila Net, for Aficionados
www.tequila.net

Spirits of Mexico
www.thespiritsofmexico.com

The Mexican Regulatory Council for Mezcal Quality/
El Consejo Mexicano Regulador de la Calidad del Mezcal
A. C. (COMERCA)
www.crm.org.mx

Promotional Council for Raicilla, the Regulatory Council
for Raicilla
www.raicillacentral.com

Puerto Vallarta Raicilla
www.puertovallarta.net

Bacanora Regulatory Council
www.facebook.com/consejoreguladordelbacanora

100 Ways to Cook with Tequila
www.endlesssimmer.com/2011/05/04/100-ways-to-cook-
with-tequila

Scorpion Mezcal Recipes
www.scorpionmezcal.com

Tequila Recipes
http://homecooking.about.com/library/archive/blalcohol1.htm

Cooking Channel
www.cookingchanneltv.com/topics/tequila.html

Acknowledgements

Writing books can be a solitary experience, but an enterprise like this depends upon the help and support of many people whose enthusiastic support made its completion possible.

No thanks at all are due to the two thugs in New York who smashed me over the head with a pistol and delayed finishing the book for year but deep appreciation for Michael Leaman at Reaktion for his understanding and support during the postponed deadline and to Marianne who helped me sort illustrations while I was still reeling with concussion.

Deep and sincere thanks to my beloved boys Owain and Ian, whose forbearance during a difficult time made the book possible. Brown Forman helped me with travel and logistics and unstintingly helped me meet people in Mexico well beyond their colleagues at Herradura, who, like all the tequila and mescal distillers, were eager to share insights and appreciation.

Dori Bryant, founder of the Spirits of Mexico, was the inspiration for the whole enterprise, but Robert Plotkin, Juan Bernardo Torres Mora, Doug French, Ron Cooper, Martin Grassl, J. P. de Loera, Jose 'Pepe' Hermosillo and Josh Wortman, along with the people from the Tequila Chamber and the Regulatory Council in Guadalajara, and many others, helped me imbibe much material for my research and share my deep appreciation.

Photo Acknowledgements

The author and publishers wish to express their thanks to the below sources of illustrative material and/or permission to reproduce it.

Photos courtesy of the author: pp. 16, 23, 27, 30, 31, 32, 34, 35, 36, 38, 40, 43, 44, 46, 52, 58, 60, 63, 64, 65, 68, 70, 77, 79, 80, 84, 86, 91, 94, 100, 106, 109, 115, 116, 118, 120, 121, 122, 125, 127, 129, 130, 133, 138; Biblioteca Nazionale Centrale, Florence: p. 53; Bodleian Library, Oxford: pp. 48, 54; British Museum, London (photo © The Trustees of the British Museum): p. 47; photo Antonio Cavallo: p. 134; photos William Henry Jackson: pp. 14, 51; Library of Congress, Washington, DC (Prints and Photographs Division): pp. 14, 51.

Germán Amaya Franky, copyright holder of the image on p. 111, Bin im Garten, the copyright holder of the image on p. 9, Castle Brands Inc., the copyright holder of the image on p. 21, and Dano Veal., the copyright holder of the image on p. 25, have published these online under conditions imposed by a Creative Commons Attribution-Share Alike 3.0 Unported license.

Under the following conditions:

attribution – readers must attribute the image in the manner specified by the author or licensor (but not in any way that suggests that these parties endorse them or their use of the work).

Index

italic numbers refer to illustrations; **bold** to recipes